# ORPHAN32

## THANH CAMPBELL

HOPE FOR THE WORLD PRODUCTIONS
www.orphan32.com

Photo Credits:
p.12-13: courtesy of Major Cliff Zacharias; p. 14: © Toronto Star; p. 20: (top) courtesy of Major Bob Nicholson, (bottom) courtesy of Major Cliff Zacharias;
p. 26, 28-29, 70-71, 103-107, 133: courtesy of Victoria Leach.

ISBN: 978-0-9936162-0-4

Design and layout: Rose Gowsell

Printed and bound in Canada.

For my children
Aaron, Matthew, Joshua, and Rachel

*This is my legacy I leave for you . . .*
*you are my legacy I leave to the World.*

This story is also dedicated to my birth family, who I never knew existed until recently. For my family in Vietnam: my father, Mr. Nguyen Minh Thanh; my mother, Mrs. Nguyen Thi Ngoc Thu (1943–1987); and my brothers, Thuan, Thao, and Thuan. I hope by telling this side of the story, you will gain a better insight to the greater purpose this painful experience had in The Great Plan.

In memory of my brother Thien (1969–2011), who leaves behind his wife and his daughter Thanh and son Thang.

In memory of Victoria Leach and Helen Allen, my heroes.

In memory of my mom, Maureen Jean Campbell (1936–2000), the best friend I have ever had.

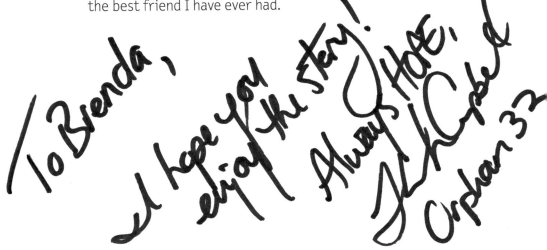

# CONTENTS

# Acknowledgements

WHEN ONE PERSON TELLS YOU TO WRITE A BOOK, IT'S A thought. When a few people tell you the same thing, you consider it. When hundreds of people tell you, it gets done. I have many people to thank for the inspiration to share my story.

I want to thank my own family: Princes Aaron, Matthew, and Joshua; my Princess Rachel; and to my wife, Karina, without whom much of this story would not have been as full or as meaningful.

To my family of which I am blessed to be a member in Canada: my dad, Reverend William Campbell; my mom, Maureen (1936–2000); my sisters, Joan and Nancy; and my brothers, Keith, Stan, and Dave — all of whom have had considerable influence on my life and helped shape me to be who I am today. And to my extended family, who was as foundational in my integration to Canada as grandparents, aunts, uncles, and cousins can be.

I am blessed with great friends, too many to list, but I would be remiss not to mention my inspirations: Jay Pluim, Keith Robinson, CJ Calvert, and Trent Kilner.

This story would not be what it is today without the media attention it received. Much appreciation to the networks and publications that covered this story: Ken Bosveld at *"The Beacon"*; Seamus, Bev, and Marci at *"Canada AM"*; Pauline Chan at *"CTV News"*; Peter Mansbridge and Melissa Fung with the *"CBC National"*; Paula Todd at "TVO"; Matt Hayes and Connie Smith at "CHCH", Lorna Dueck at "CTS", George McEachern, Moira Brown, and the team at *"100 Huntley Street"*; Journalist Jordan Heath Rawlings; Dana Robbins and Jane Allison at *TorStar* and all their affiliates; Shelley Page from *The Ottawa Sun*; Redeemer University College's Images, and finally Ms. Thanh Truc of *Tuoi Tre* newspaper in Ho Chi Minh City.

I would also like to add a special thank you to my editing team of Nancy Whytock, Carla Whytock, Carrie Gleason, Greg Hatton and Naomi Biesheuvel. Thanks also goes to my creative team, David Hills and the team at CanWeb Printing, and especially to Rose Gowsell of Plan B Book Packagers without you, this book would never have seen the light of day.

Above all, I would like to give thanks to God, who gave me life itself and the story to share.

# Foreword

**WHEN I FIRST ARRIVED IN CANADA I COULD HAVE BEEN THE** poster child for any relief organization. Malnutrition impacts people throughout their lives, especially when they lived in its grip for the first few years. Being deprived of essential nutrients when the body is forming impedes development at a crucial stage in life. In my case, this means poor dental health, liver and digestive troubles, and chronic ear infections to this day.

Having visited Vietnam in 2009 and seeing poverty reign to this day, I get troubled in my spirit as to how much still is needed to be done globally to combat poverty. I got this same sense having done mission work with World Vision. I have seen a glimpse of what life continues to be like in the developing world. I have witnessed the impact of poverty and how it ravages a life, a community, a nation.

I was in Haiti in 1995 and then again in 2011. On my first trip in 1995, our team was travelling to a Baptist Mission in the mountains. As we travelled the roads to the highlands, we had to go through a coastal area that had rice paddies on either side of the road. Even though we were in

Haiti, I had an eerie feeling of familiarity come over me, like déjà vu. I believe I even saw people in the fields with those cone-shaped hats. It felt like I was in a flashback scene of a Vietnam War movie and I was waiting to see a Huey drop out of the sky.

I realized how much I related to these people who are so oppressed by poverty. It was so long ago that I had been airlifted out of that life and saved to live a privileged life in Canada. I had to ask myself *"What was the purpose of it all? Why was I blessed to escape?"*

It amazed me, both times I visited Haiti, that people who live in such poverty can even function daily and be "happy." It was a humbling experience.

When I returned in 2011 I was so impressed with the work and the hope that World Vision brings to places like this in the world. I have included an opportunity in the back of this book that opens the door to people to offer help to a child in need.

People are moved emotionally by what these children must endure. Sometimes it is overwhelming to think that there are so many children in need in so many countries. I know people think, *I am just one person, I can't do everything for everybody*. The need is so great and it is easy to feel helpless about making a real difference. My response is to start with helping one. Make a difference in one life and feel the difference in your own.

For much less than a price of a cup of coffee, a child's life can be rescued from an early death or lingering health issues caused by malnutrition.

I don't believe organizations like World Vision get started because someone had a great idea about helping children in need. I believe it happens because somewhere out there a mother, a father, or a grandmother cries out with a prayer for help. The seed of an answer to that prayer gets planted into the heart of someone who will respond to the call for help. **Whose answer to prayer will you be?**

Thank you for your support, you are making a difference!

**PART ONE**

# FLIGHT TO FREEDOM
Saigon to Toronto
April 1975

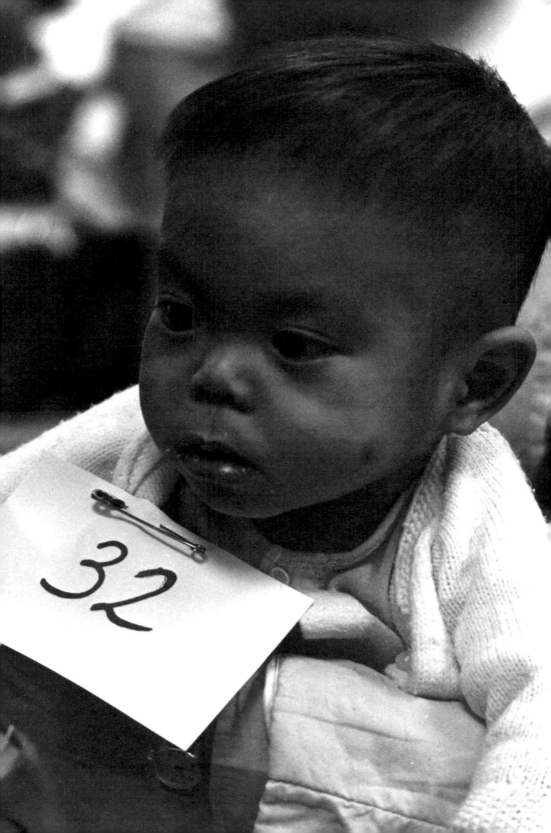

chapter 1
# Beginnings

**I DON'T CLAIM TO BE A HISTORIAN, YET IN ORDER TO** share my story, I thought it might help if I set the context of the era in which I was born.

The Vietnam War started in 1954. It was a civil war that was to reunify the Southeast Asian country of Vietnam. Ho Chi Minh was a communist dictator who wanted to subdue the democratic republic to the south. The conflict escalated to the point where the Americans joined the South Vietnamese effort in 1964 during the Tet Offensive, which was named for the time of year it was being fought. The Season of Tet is during the month of January and is more commonly known in other parts of the world as the Chinese New Year. It is a time of celebration and bringing families together, but the war was leaving little to celebrate and caused the separation of many families.

As the conflict escalated, it became very clear that the North Vietnamese Army was advancing and gaining ground. In response, the United States Armed Forces had to learn to build a military strategy to fight in an environment they were not used to fighting in.

As is the case in so many wars, there was great

collateral damage that extended beyond just the physical destruction of the landscape. Records show that during the Vietnam War more bombs were dropped on this tiny sliver of coastal land in the South Pacific than during both World Wars put together — and the land would never recover. Society broke down and the South Vietnamese who were able began to make evacuation plans in case the worst should happen and the country be reunified under Ho Chi Minh and his Communist Regime.

Families were being ripped apart and many children were orphaned. The people of South Vietnam didn't have access to the community services from which I have come to benefit by living in Canada. Often, the only option for a single mother being crushed by poverty was to abandon her baby. Many did so, leaving their children to die in the streets, dumps, or burned-out villages. Other parents, who did not have the heart to do this, left their children to be cared for by Catholic nuns who started taking in abandoned infants. These care facilities quickly grew in number as the war continued. Some babies were left on the doorsteps of Catholic churches or orphanages, while others were given directly to the headmistress to be cared for indefinitely. No matter how you say it, these kids were being abandoned with the hope that they would be provided for and given a better life.

At that time, an organization called Friends For All was monitoring what was happening to these infants. With the inevitability of the Communist occupation of Saigon, they knew what would happen to these orphans: they would be killed or left to die. According to those that worked in the country at the time, the illegitimate children of American

G.I.'s — who had abandoned both mother and child — were at even more risk.

Knowing this to be the fate of these young people, Friends For All started making plans to save them. It took a lot of calls and political finesse to get the message out to country leaders, but the effort was worth it in the end. Messages were wired to governments of the first-world nations near and far; a plea to take these orphans into their care and to place them in loving homes to be cherished and cared for the rest of their lives.

Once the story was broadcast over the media in these countries, hearts were moved. Australia, the United Kingdom, and later the United States came to the aid of the child advocacy group in South Vietnam to evacuate the children.

## Falling From the Sky

**IN APRIL 1975, AN AMERICAN MILITARY LOCKHEED GALAXY** C5 cargo plane loaded with toddlers and their caregivers flew out of Tan Son Nhat Airport in Saigon, headed for the United States. This was a flight of a larger rescue mission called Operation Babylift that had gained worldwide notice and criticism. While many people felt compassion for the kids who were affected by the war, people debated whether or not children ought to be taken from their country of birth.

As the aircraft made its ascent, the plane experienced mechanical failures and the door to the rear fuselage blew open. The aircraft immediately lost cabin pressure and the plane started to go down. The pilots tried to gain control of the damaged aircraft and head back to the landing strip. While still on course for the runway, the plane descended too quickly for the pilots to safely maneuver it, and the plane crashed. Smoke from the wreckage could be seen for many miles. Of the 313 passengers onboard, just 175 survived. Vietnamese media reported that the plane was brought down due to mechanical failure, but there is speculation that it was shot at and took a direct hit, causing the door to be unhinged and thus the deadly descent to begin Nothing has been officially documented. Nevertheless, the urgency to rescue more children was heightened in light of this tragedy.

## O Canada

**THE CANADIAN GOVERNMENT RESPONDED TO THE** original call for help to take the remaining children. The government stipulated that any child who came had to be proven to be a true orphan; meaning there was no possibility of parents coming to reclaim the child after the war. Another organization, Friends of the Children of Vietnam, agreed to the conditions and started selecting children from different orphanages.

Throughout the spring of 1975, Victoria Leach, head of the Ministry of Community and Social Services for the Province of Ontario, and Helen Allen, her co-leader, had made several trips to Vietnam to bring back one or two orphans at a time for adoption by Canadian families. Spurred on by the Galaxy Crash, they planned one last rescue mission. This group would be their biggest so far:

500 Vietnamese orphans. A team of volunteers, doctors and nurses, and government officials were assembled to help.

The organizers, along with the help of the group Friends of the Children of Vietnam, had gathered the orphans from outlying areas and brought them to the Go Vap Orphanage in Saigon. When Victoria and Helen's team arrived in Saigon, the orphanage directors could only prove that 57 of the children were true orphans. Each child was assigned a number and a volunteer care worker with the same number, so that anything communicable would not be transferred amongst the group. An infant named Nguyen Ngoc Minh Thanh was given the number 32.

I was Orphan 32, and this is my story.

Major Bob Nicholson

Crew of Service Flight 515 from Trenton, Ontario.

## chapter 2
# Flight of the Orphans

**THE NEXT HURDLE VICTORIA LEACH HAD TO FACE WAS** finding a way to transport the orphans out of the country via a commercial or military flight. A message was wired to Hong Kong, requesting help from any available aircraft. Fortunately, at that time, the Canadian Air Force was running training flights for their Hercules C130 planes out of CFB Trenton, Ontario, to Hong Kong. When the training instructor, Captain Cliff Zacharias, arrived in Hong Kong, he saw all of his planes still parked on the runway. He stormed into the office and was ready to discipline his trainees for disobeying orders and not going back to Canada. One brave crew member informed the captain that they were being commissioned to fly in and get Victoria and her team out. They also had to come up with a way to accommodate the orphans while transporting them out of harm's way.

The captain, Lieutenant Bob Nicholson, and crew flew from Hong Kong to Tan Son Nhat Airport in Saigon, and waited for Victoria Leach and her team to arrive with their cargo. Flying into that airport was no easy feat, considering the conditions facing them at that point in the Vietnam conflict and in the shadow of the Galaxy Crash.

Communication was sent to the Go Vap Orphanage to let

them know that the plane was ready for them. The team began to assemble the orphans and load them into vans, which would taxi them to the airport. But when the caravan left the gates of the orphanage it was slowed by the mayhem of citizens scrambling to get out of a capital city on the edge of doom.

At the airport, the vans headed directly for the back of the terminal and through the gates that lead to the runway. As the vans rounded the corner, their "knights in military-green armour" were waiting to whisk the children away to safety. This was new territory for these aviators, accustomed to transporting military gear and personnel. Instead of tanks, ammunition, or supplies, inside the hull of this massive airliner were rows of empty cardboard cartons. With the plane's tail open and the ramp lowered, the flight crew began loading their "cargo" into the hull of the plane.

The infants were placed in the cardboard boxes, sometimes more than one to a box. Toddlers were settled along the walls of the aircraft. The ages of the children ranged from three months to nine years old. All of them were seriously malnourished and underweight; some suffering from tuberculosis, intestinal parasites, or malaria. Others had been physically wounded during the war.

Once the orphans were placed in their travel positions, a frantic Victoria Leach approached the cockpit to alert the captain of a new development. South Vietnamese army personnel had boarded the plane and were demanding to see the official papers that coincided with the number of children being taken out, and they were one short. "Over my dead body will they take one of my children off this plane," Victoria Leach told the pilot. Captain Cliff Zacharias ordered his lieutenant and friend, Bob Nicholson, to fire up the engines and prepare for take-off. Then he grabbed his captain's hat and gave his second order, to Victoria Leach, telling her to take her seat. The Captain took a deep breath and started toward the South Vietnamese soldiers, waving his arms with an air of impatience. "Hong Kong is closing, Hong Kong is closing!" he shouted. With his every step the soldiers retreated until they were past the threshold of the tailgate. Seeing his opportunity, Captain Zacharias ordered the doors closed. He quickly returned to his seat at the helm, offering up a quick prayer of thanks. It would not be his last on this mission.

The Hercules C130 was a massive construct of aviation engineering designed to transport military goods. Usually in this type of scenario, fighter jets would be scrambled as escorts, but there would be no such cover provided on this day. The responsibility of all the lives on board fell squarely on the shoulders of the Canadian airmen who had risked life and limb to whisk the lucky few they had just met to a different destiny than their country mates who were left behind.

The pilot and crew relied heavily on their training in evasive maneuvers and understood the deadly consequences of taking too much ground fire. Captain Zacharias knew he had a small margin for error. He was accustomed to having a good long runway to reach the speed needed to provide enough lift on take-off, as well as a longer measure of post runway clearance to climb at a gradual incline so that the weight of the load would not shift. This was not a luxury afforded to them this day. It would have challenged any top gun pilot. Their lives literally hung in the balance.

The C130 Hercules plane lifted off very quickly and in a corkscrew pattern, circling higher and higher, and eventually gained enough lift to avoid the ground fire from the Viet Cong — South Vietnam supporters of the Communist Regime. Even though bullets from anti-aircraft artillery were hitting the hull of the plane, they never penetrated, and missiles exploded short distances from the fuselage. It was as if an unseen hand of protection surrounded the plane like bubble wrap, encasing the precious cargo. Once a safe flying altitude was reached, the aircraft set its course for Hong Kong. Its passengers and crew never looked back.

## A Lot of TLC

IMMEDIATELY AFTER LANDING AT THE HONG KONG airport, the passengers were whisked not to a hospital or local medical clinic, but to a makeshift care centre atop a luxury hotel. The volunteers from the first leg of the trip were given respite while a team of doctors and nurses who had been commissioned as triage units to take care of the orphans took over. For two days they worked around the clock to tend to the malnourished and ill-fated children, who were stricken with polio, Hepatitis A and B, scabies, intestinal parasites, diarrhea, and a whole host of other unpleasant and potentially communicable diseases.

In order to be allowed into Canada, each child had to be inoculated for TB, measles, mumps, and other diseases. Once all shots were given, fifty-five orphans were given clearance to continue on to North America. Two of them were too sick to travel right away and were held back to be nursed back to a measurable level of health before continuing on their journey to the Promised Land.

A Canadian Pacific Airways transpacific flight from Hong

Kong to Vancouver, B.C., was taken over by Victoria Leach, her team, and her children. It was a much less eventful flight over the Pacific, but when the plane landed in Vancouver on April 12, 1975, it taxied into a media scrum waiting to get their first shots of the "Asian babies" rescued from war.

It was a moment that would not soon be forgotten. TV reporters in front of their cameras shared the story of the orphans' plight and the heroic efforts of those who put themselves at risk to take them out of war ravaged South Vietnam.

After a night's layover, the orphans were boarded onto an Air Canada domestic flight to Pearson International Airport in Toronto, with a stopover in Calgary. Fifty-three orphans carried on with this leg of the journey; two flight mates were left in the West. Where they ended up, nobody knows at this point. There is speculation that they were survivors of the Galaxy Crash and were headed for a connecting flight to the United States where their adoptive parents had been anxiously waiting for them. There is a chance that they were adopted by families in British Columbia. All that is known for certain is that their journey with the original "57 Orphans" had come to an end.

Toronto-bound passengers helped care for the remaining orphans. One child was put into the arms of an anonymous oil tycoon from Alberta. When the executive's stop came in Calgary, he did not relinquish his "package" but insisted on seeing the child to Ontario, only booking his return flight once he knew his child had reached his final destination.

I like to believe this gentleman would have done this whether he could have afforded to or not, stirred on by a strong sense of goodwill.

Mrs. Victoria Leach, Adoption Co-ordinator for Ontario, with children in a Saigon orphanage. All the boys and girls seen here have had polio. Some of the children were supplied with braces, mostly gifts received from the U.S., but no treatment was available in the way of physiotherapy or surgery.

Orphan 32

PEDIATRIC SURGERY  *Michael S. Allen*  MD FRCS/C FAAP

SUITE 210 / 658 COXWELL AVENUE
TORONTO 13 / ONTARIO / 466-1220

Mr. Rene Brunelle,
Minister of Community and Social Services,
Hepburn Building,
Queens Park, Toronto

Re: <u>Mrs. Victoria Leach</u>

Dear Mr. Brunelle:

Having just returned from Saigon and Hong Kong with the
Vietnamese air lift of children, I wish personally to note the
excellent co-ordination and leadership of Mrs. Leach. Despite
long hours, short periods of sleep, and ill health from gastro-
enteritis contracted in Saigon, she continued in control of this
exodus from beginning to end. Because of diplomatic protocol, the
légation in Saigon could offer little help and hence almost single
handedly she sought out the children, saw that they were fed,
treated medically and then brought safely to Hong Kong. Her arrange-
ments with the federal representatives in Hong Kong could only be
described as superb, and I will be forever grateful for being a
part of her team.

The whole endeavour may only be a drop in the bucket in easing
the frightful conditions in South Viet Nam but perhaps it is a step
in the right direction in bringing home to Canadians the result of
war and in making the universal skin colour beige.

With kindest regards,

Michael S. Allen, F.R.C.S.(C)
April 15, 1975

MSA/kw

**PART TWO**

# FROM SURREY PLACE AND BACK AGAIN

Toronto
April 17, 1975 to April 2006

Rev. William Campbell

Maureen Jean Campbell

# chapter 3
# The Call That Started it All

ON APRIL 17, 1975, REVEREND WILLIAM CAMPBELL AND HIS wife Maureen were attending a wedding of one of their congregants in Cambridge, Ontario. At home in Galt, their eldest daughter, Joan, was left in charge of her younger siblings, Nancy, Stanley, and David.

The phone rang during suppertime. Joan greeted the caller. The voice on the other end said: "Are you still interested in adopting one of the Vietnamese children that just arrived?" It was a call the Campbell family had been waiting — and praying — for.

A few months earlier, the news had hit the airwaves that the Canadian government was considering opening its doors to Vietnamese war children. At that time, many people were opposed to America's involvement in the war. Even the idea of taking children out of the war-torn country evoked strong debate on both sides of the border between Canada and United States. Stories had surfaced that custody battles were emerging in the United States where Vietnamese parents had somehow tracked down their children who had been evacuated and placed for adoption. The birth parents made heart-wrenching legal claims against well-meaning adoptive families who had just been blessed with a new son or daughter that they were quietly knitting into the fabric of their American lives. Now the adoptive families stood helplessly by as the children were taken from their homes and placed into foster care as wards of the state until the cases could be settled. The Canadian government would have no part in that type of conflict and made the organizers of Operation Babylift prove that the children who arrived in Canada were true orphans. This was difficult to prove, so the coordinators in Vietnam selected the children who would be allowed to leave; they chose the ones who had been transferred from outlying orphanages.

While reading an article about Operation Babylift in the Cambridge newspaper, Maureen Campbell had felt a maternal pull inside her, one she had had before. The previous year, she had read Helen Allen's weekly feature entitled "Today's Child," which showcased local children who were available for adoption. This is how Maureen and her husband, William, had already come to adopt two of their sons, Stanley (Portuguese-Italian) and David (Trinidadian-Jamaican).

But something in Maureen, a stay-at-home mom, made her consider the possibility of bringing yet another child into this already busy family. She mentioned it to her husband, and it was mutually acceptable to him. As the spiritual leader in his community and family, William lived by the saying that his "walk should match his talk," and shortly after this he left the pastoral ministry and pursued a career with World Vision Canada.

Maureen Campbell let the idea simmer for a while. As

a devout Christian, she wanted to ensure that the decision was not emotionally driven, but rather divinely ordained. After a week or so passed with the couple's dedication to commit this to their already extensive prayer list, a definitive answer was planted in each of their hearts: yes, they would open their home to yet another child, should they be accepted by the adoption agency.

With the decision made, they made the call to the Ministry of Community and Family Services, which had also facilitated their previous two adoptions. In speaking with the case manager, who was familiar with the Campbell family, they received the hesitant response that, "because they waited, there was now a waiting list of families that had expressed interest and they had to be put at the bottom of it." They agreed to wait.

Life went on for the Campbells. There was no shortage of responsibilities: children to be cared for, school teams to support, newspaper routes to cover, and weddings of congregants to attend.

About a month later, when Joan answered the call, she assured the caller that yes, her family was still interested in adopting one of the children and that they would come to Toronto the next day to pick up the child.

Joan went to work and immediately enlisted the help of her younger siblings to ready their home for another new sibling; this time it would be an infant. While her sister and brothers were busy with their assigned tasks, Joan called her parents at the wedding reception. Reverend William took the call. After learning the news, he returned to the table and let his wife finish her dessert before giving her the news. Just as he expected, as soon as she heard, she insisted they leave for home immediately.

By the time Maureen and William arrived home, the children had cleaned the entire house and set up the nursery. For the members of the Campbell family, that long night was filled with a fitful sleep — the same kind one has before a birthday or Christmas. The next day, they would be making the hour-long trip to Surrey Place Centre in Toronto to meet the newest member of their family.

chapter 4
# Surrey Place

**SURREY PLACE CENTRE AT 1 SURREY PLACE, TORONTO,** Ontario, was chosen as the first Canadian home of the latest Vietnamese orphans. Usually the facility was used for special-needs children and their families for rehabilitation classes and therapy. Surrey Place Centre is located around the corner from the Hospital for Sick Children, making it ideal for the orphans who would require special medical care.

As Victoria was preparing to leave for Vietnam, a call for volunteers had been sent out to the community to support the effort with the Government's Department of Family and Community Services. It was met with a resounding show of support and people registered to volunteer and assist these newcomers upon their arrival. What had been a day-program facility would now be a twenty-four-hour intensive care/adoption centre for these needy children.

In preparation, a nursery was built for the infants and a special ward assembled to house the toddlers and older children. Beds were placed into rows and columns, dormitory-style. The top two floors of the facility would be home to the children for nine months.

Dr. Pratrap Rastogi was the lead family physician preparing the Toronto medical community to receive the orphans. Under his direction, a team of various specialists in tropical diseases, nutrition, rehabilitation, and other child ailments was quickly assembled.

Social workers and adoption officers had been working for months to arrange for welcoming homes in which the children would be placed. Lawyers and immigration specialists worked long hours to ensure smooth transitions for the adoptive parents to assimilate these new members into their families. Most parents, like the Campbells, had already been through the approval process for interracial adoptions.

At the grassroots level, the families reached out to their relatives, friends, and support communities to rally around them in order to provide the support one needs when taking in a foreign child.

Upon the orphans' arrival, Surrey Place volunteers were the primary caregivers who first got to know them. Infants, such as myself, were taken care of in the nursery on the second floor and toddlers and older children on the third level. Volunteers who worked the night shift reported that in the middle of the night, older children pushed the beds together so they were all touching. The younger children slept in the middle with the older ones on the outside for protection.

During the day, the older children squirrelled away extra food and snacks in their mattresses. At night, the food was shared with the younger ones. The volunteers witnessed this, but did not disturb the practice.

This was not how things had been for the children back in Vietnam. There, it had been survival of the fittest. Children had hoarded food in the orphanages due to the food scarcity. Stockpiles of food were protected in a mob-like manner, without allowing the weaker or younger children access to it. Those caught stealing food were often beaten by the caregivers. The need to survive was so strong that the stealing and hoarding continued. Something changed in the children when they got to Canada, and instead of seeing one another as competition, they were now cohorts.

Even infants such as myself did not escape this scarcity mentality. When I first arrived in the Campbell home it was very uncommon for me to have any "leftovers," unlike children who had grown up on three meals a day.

To test the boundaries of our new relationship, my brother Dave, who was five at the time, would tease me by pretending he was going to steal the food from my highchair tray. Despite scolding from our mother, Dave would continue this game until I would start snarling — a low growling sound, my sisters say.

My father claims he knew I had transitioned out of this a year later, when we went to McDonald's and I left half a hamburger behind to play in the Playland. I was now a normal child that was secure, knowing that there was not a scarcity of food in this new world. Food waste would not be tolerated much more after then.

## chapter 5
# Early Years

**EVEN THOUGH MY BROTHER DAVE AND I WERE TWO OF THE** few non-white students at Cambridge Christian School, we were treated no differently than anyone else and welcomed into this mostly Dutch school.

However, I knew my story of coming to Canada interested people, as my parents would share it with their house guests, or I would share it in my show-and-tell times in elementary school.

The community in which I grew up made me feel special — not odd — for having this story that was unique. I suppose this is why I became adept at sharing it, almost proud. But when I would look at books about the Vietnam War and saw some of the horrific pictures taken by American journalists, I would close the book quickly, as though it was a type of Pandora's box that would open some dark nightmare in my psyche. When our family sponsored some of the Vietnamese "Boat People" in 1978, it was the closest thing to having that box ripped open in my young life.

When I was first adopted, the local newspaper came to my parents asking for an interview. My father was a prominent pastor in the area with his own local religious TV program. He was sure that they were going to try to make it look like he did this as a PR thing. By refusing the interview, he wanted to make it clear that adopting a Vietnam War orphan was a private personal choice of his and his wife's and not something for which he wanted to be praised in the media .

## The Letter

**SHORTLY AFTER I WAS ADOPTED, MY SISTER JOAN HAD** written a letter to Victoria Leach, the director of the Ministry of Community and Family Services at the time, to find out the details of her new little brother's evacuation from Vietnam. Not intimidated by Victoria Leach's title and position in the government, nor her own status in life, she wanted to leave no stone unturned in her research. This letter began a butterfly effect that, many years down the road, created a flood of activity that led to this book being written.

Victoria held on to Joan's letter for a long time, but eventually it was discarded. Yet Victoria's three-page letter of reply was never thrown out, and it has been a cornerstone on which this story was built as it is a detailed account of the flight from Vietnam.

Ontario

Ministry of
Community and
Social
Services

Parliament Buildings
Queen's Park
Toronto Ontario
M7A 1E9

September 27, 1977

.Miss Joan Campbell,
650 Grant Ridge Dr.,
Cambridge, Ontario.
N1S 4J8

Dear Miss Campbell:

Thank you for your letter of September 19th telling
me of your hope to put together a history of little Thanh's
journey to Canada from Vietnam - what a nice sister you are.
I am sure as he grows older, he will appreciate this even more.

I will try to fill in the missing blanks from memory.

This Ministry had been sending home studies of families hoping to adopt Vietnamese children from Vietnam for
several years before the air lift. In fact, in July of 1973
Helen Allen, our Adoption Information Officer and I journeyed
to Vietnam to meet with officials there to see if it would be
possible for our families to adopt some of their children and
to give the authorities there the assurance that our Ministry
would see that the children were cared for (see attached report). Following that trip, a number of children did come
out to Ontario families.

In February of 1975, I went back to Vietnam again and
again indicated that our families were prepared to accept and
love these little people, many of whom had never known a family.
Some of them were abandoned at orphanage gates, others were
left in churches and hotel lobbies or on Embassy steps. I
also wanted to see if the authorities would be willing to let
the children out prior to the adoption being completed in the
Vietnamese Courts, which they were insisting on at that time.

On my return trip, I brought nine children back with
me and their new families met them at the airport. It was a
very long trip - we flew from Saigon to Manilla, then into Guam,
then to Hawaii, then to San Francisco, up to Vancouver and home
to Toronto. The kids were good little travellers. We spent
one night in Honolulu, but all in all, we had twenty six hours
in the air.

In April of 1975, our Ministry received a telegram
from "Friends For All Children", an agency we had been working with, asking us if we could place 500 babies. We wired back

that we would come over with a team of doctors and nurses if necessary. They wired back "Come as soon as possible" - within days we left with a nurse, two doctors, Helen Allen and myself.

Between the time that we took off and the time we got there, a large American C5 aircraft, taking children out to the United States, crashed and many of the children were killed, as well as a number of the staff of the agency. In the shock and grief that followed, the remaining staff arranged for children to be placed on aircraft going to any country that would accept them as quickly as possible. When our team finally got there, we found there were very few children left. We did get in touch with a Dutch priest, Father Peter Aarts, whom I had met in February and who also knew other Canadians who had been there and were interested in adoptions. Father Aarts offered to assist us and did take a van into an orphanage located almost in the enemy territory - brought out a number of children and took them to a place called "Friends of the Children of Vietnam" located in the middle of Saigon. In addition, one of the largest orphanages there named Go-Vap, run by the Roman Catholic nuns, allowed us to take about twenty babies to the same place. At that time, we still had a Canadian Charge' D'Affairs there, a young, dedicated man named Ernest Hebert. He processed the necessary paper work to allow the children into Canada and also negotiated with the Vietnamese to provide passports or other necessary permits to leave Vietnam as quickly as possible.

Our team in Vietnam was one doctor and Helen Allen and myself. I am a registered nurse as well as a professional social worker. Dr. Ward examined all the children, in fact he stayed with them all night because some of the children were ill. Dr. Michael Allen, a Pediatric Surgeon, and Elizabeth Ralph, the nurse-social worker, stayed in Hong Kong and set up a receiving centre on the 17th floor of the Plaza Hotel there, along with very able help from the embassy wives who were in that city.

On the day of departure, Mr. Hebert arranged for a bus and a number of cars and we were escorted to the airport where a Canadian Armed Forces Hercules Cargo Aircraft was waiting for us. We all piled on and the young airmen all assisted us. The babies were in cardboard boxes strapped to the floor, two babies to a box. The older ones sat in seats around the edges of the aircraft. We had bottles of water and sugar and juices and cookies for the older ones. It was a four and a half hour flight to Hong Kong. When we got to the airport there, the authorities held us until we could prove all the children were vaccinated. Those without proof were vaccinated right in the airport, before we could move. We were then put on a special bus and taken to the Plaza, where a wonderful group of volunteers met us. It was a luxurious hotel and there was a volunteer for every three children. The doctors checked the little ones again and they were all bathed, changed and fed and put to bed.

We had arrived in Hong Kong on a Friday evening and we left there on Sunday noon. Two of the children were not well enough to travel so we arranged for them to be admitted to hospital and they came to Canada a little later.

We left Hong Kong by CP Air, stopped briefly in Toyko, and then onto Vancouver where we were met by staff of the Department of Human Resources who gave the escorts a break of two hours while they took over. We changed to Air Canada in Vancouver and flew directly to Toronto where we were met by our own Ministry officials and the children were taken directly to Surrey Place Centre.

Besides our own team, we had a number of other volunteers from Hong Kong and the other passengers were wonderful in helping us. We were exhausted and the Surrey Place staff took over. It was there that you and your family went to meet little Than . Every child was examined carefully and checked for parasites in the bowel or any other condition which might affect him or his new family.

Our Ministry did put together a film based on movies that Helen and I arranged when we were in Vietnam in 1973. It is called 25,000 orphans. It shows a number of scenes of the orphanages and gives you a little idea of the country. We would be glad to lend it to you if you'd like to see it. It is on 16 mm film so if you have or can borrow a 16 mm projector, you could see it. I am also enclosing some of my photos of the orphanages in Saigon so you can have them for Thank's memory book.

Many families and social workers make scrapbooks for adoptees. You could get a picture of a Hercules Aircraft, CP Air 747 and an Air Canada 747 and one of Surrey Place, I am sure.

Once again I'd like to commend you for taking time to write to me to gather information for your little brother. I would be interested to know a little about you. You write so beautifully. Please call me at 965-2802 if there are any other questions.

Most sincerely yours,

Victoria Leach
Adoption Co-ordinator.

VL./lmc
Encl.

# Misconceptions — Would the Real Me Please Step Forward?

**MY FAMILY LEFT ONTARIO TO MOVE TO NEW BRUNSWICK IN** 1981. It was a hard transition, leaving family and friends. Even though we lived in the countryside just outside of Cambridge, Ontario, we had the best of both worlds — city life and rural retreat. I didn't know what to expect moving to the Maritimes. It didn't help that my brother David said that all there is to do in the Maritimes was to be a woodsman or a fisherman. I envisioned us living in a shack in the woods and having to walk to the village to get on our fishing boat. Needless to say, I suffered through the long trip in our family station wagon from Cambridge to Moncton thinking about how I was going to grow up to become a lumberjack.

Arriving in Moncton, we discovered it was a very urban area. We lived in a suburb called Riverview, and while my brothers went to middle school in the city, I finished elementary school at Lower Coverdale Elementary School. It was a small country school with a wonderful, welcoming community feel to it; very much like my former school, Cambridge Christian School in Ontario.

In grade seven I transitioned to Riverview Junior High School, which was a bigger, urban school. Then I graduated to the even bigger Riverview High School with over a thousand students. Even though I got involved with school activities like band and the track-and-field team, I felt lost and very much alone. My insecurities got the best of me and I found myself caught up in trying to fit in with my peers, while at the same time trying to present myself as a respectable pastor's kid.

Throughout my high school years, I felt I was on a

mission to try to figure out who I really was. Not who I thought I wanted to be, or what others thought of me, but who I *really* was. Although most teens deal with this as part of the self-actualization process, I felt for me it was different. For the most part, my peers knew their parents, they knew where they were born, and they knew their medical history. Being adopted, I had no connection to my heritage. The only resource I had at my disposal to guide me was the way I felt according to each experience; I had to "trust" my inner feelings.

Even though I was brought up in a religious home, I did not fully grasp the understanding of a god that would interact with me. Instead, I had a more distant connection and viewed Him more as a judge who sat up "on high" and who was waiting for me to mess up. I did not put my trust in Him, rather I feared him and what he thought of me, whoever "I" was.

I did not trust anyone else with my deepest feelings, especially about my adoption. I felt somewhat like a ticking time bomb with my real feelings suppressed. I felt very alone in this great big world. At the same time, however, I was good at keeping a very amicable exterior, but inside, a great battle was being waged.

I developed a trust issue — trust in myself. Sometimes I would think or do things that I knew deep down were not right, but I would do them anyway. It was like couldn't even live up to the moral code I had set for myself. For the most part, I was left trusting my gut feeling, even though I knew how deceptive feelings could be. It was like an internal checklist that I would score myself upon. Learning about who I was and what I liked would come down to how I felt about things. *What else did I have to go on?*

This inner conflict caused me a lot of grief and moved

me to do a lot of introspection. I was awkwardly making my way through adolescence while still trying to understand what this void was in my life. When I was thirteen years old, I was going through my photo albums and personal files my mother had collected for me over the years — mementoes, elementary-school class pictures, etc. On one of her visits from Ontario, my sister Joan handed me a package of information with some pictures in it. As I sorted through the package, I found documents about Vietnam, a short story written by her titled "Five O'Clock Follies: Effects of the Vietnam War on the Vietnamese" (based on news reports of the same name), and a letter from the government signed by a lady named Victoria Leach. There was also an adoption certificate and two copies of a birth certificate — one in Vietnamese and one in English. Using the information Leach provided, Joan's research paper theorized how baby Thanh made it to the Go Vap Orphanage.

As I looked at the different names and places on the birth certificate, I thought about the hospital where was born. It was in a place called Phuoc Tuy. I looked at a globe — these were the days before the Internet — but it was not there. Next I found an atlas and looked at a map of Vietnam. I found Saigon (now called Ho Chi Minh City), and started scanning around the map for Phuoc Tuy. But nothing close to that name was near Saigon. I went to the outlying areas and I found it! Phuoc Tuy is a province east of Saigon, in a region called Ba Ria/Vung Tau on the South China Sea. Even though it was just some place on a map, I was very excited to locate the place where I was born.

Excitement turned to curiosity and I started to wonder how I had ended up in an orphanage in Saigon if the hospital where I was born was a hundred kilometres away. I had heard stories of how kids were left at the doorstep of churches and orphanages, others were found in burned-out villages, and some were even left to die by the side of the road. Surely I was not one of those kids; I had identification papers. So how then, had I ended up at an orphanage in Saigon?

I asked my mom, "Having been born way over here..." — pointing to Phuoc Tuy on the map — "...how did I end up there?" — pointing to Saigon.

Searching for the right words, she said: "Thanh, it is time that you know that these papers are most likely not your own . . ."

My immediate reaction was of shock and bewilderment. How could this be? They had always called me Thanh, which matched the name on these papers and everything else that came with me when I was adopted…

She then shared with me the information that Victoria Leach had given them when I first arrived. The fact was, just because papers were associated with an orphan when they arrived in Canada, it did not necessarily mean they belonged to that child. In order to be allowed to leave the country, official government documents — either a birth certificate or some type of identification papers — had to accompany each child; even if they weren't really a match. We have come to find out that some of the papers were from children that had died; others may have even belonged to a child that was left behind in the orphanage.

"You mean my name isn't really Thanh?" I asked.

"You'll always be Thanh to us and that's all that matters, right?" my mom quickly tried to reassure me.

I knew what she meant, and that she meant well, but something did not sit right with me after that. My heart sank and my mind started to whirl. My thoughts started to spin in my head: *A name is how human beings are identified, if you don't have a name, how do you exist? It's like being called Baby X.* I was nameless. I had no real identification. I felt like a lost soul, wandering around trying to find something solid to possess. *If I was not Thanh, then who was I?* That was the only way people had ever known me. I was the kid with the cute dimples and unique name, hard to pronounce, but once you got it, it was hard to forget. I had spent so much time explaining to others how to pronounce my name, and now it wasn't even mine. Bizarre thoughts plagued me: *What if I get to heaven and I meet the real Thanh, Would he be angry that I was using his name all this time?*

Though this was the start of an identity crisis, I was thirteen and I was able to put it aside and get distracted in other areas of my teen angst. But somewhere in the back of my mind, finding out my real name plagued me. I wanted to get to the bottom of it.

## What's in a Name?

**THAT SUMMER, I GOT TO TRAVEL ALONE TO SCOTLAND TO** visit my sister Nancy and her husband, Jack, who was studying at the University of Glasgow. We had an amazing experience during those three weeks. One of the most important moments for me was visiting Inveraray Castle, the ancestral home of the Campbell clan. Even though I did not have the Campbell bloodline in me, I felt as much like a Campbell as anyone else with the last name; so I signed the family guest book. I am sure it was a funny scene seeing a Vietnamese guy signing a Scottish family registry, but at that point, I was starting to understand that family membership goes beyond shared genes.

Later that summer, I had the opportunity to attend

Atlantic Pioneer Camp in Prince Edward Island. It was good to get away from the city and the peer pressure I was experiencing. While I was there, I did some further searching in my heart as to the meaning of life . . . and death. One night after campfire I was moved emotionally by the message and I was encouraged to say the Sinner's Prayer and accept Jesus into my heart. I was not fully aware of what that meant, even though I had grown up in the church. To be honest, it was not that I was putting my trust in God; for me, it was the decision that I did not want to go to Hell forever. If that's what it took to seal the deal, I wanted to make sure I was on the right side. At camp I had made the decision to be a Christ follower, not for its rewards, but more because I didn't want to experience the alternative.

After summer, school started and the same patterns in life seemed to emerge. My trust in people deteriorated even more. It was similar to *The Great Sadness* described in Wm. Paul Young's book *The Shack*. It was like a shroud that was quickly enfolding me or dark waters that never let me surface no matter how much I tried to fight to keep my head above water.

I remember lying on my bed asking God to take me away from this world of loneliness. I was consumed with the thought that no one will ever "get me." *If they really knew who I was, they wouldn't do things that would betray me or hurt my feelings*. I didn't just want God to take away the feeling of being empty or lost, I wanted Him to take me away, to leave this life and be in Heaven if it meant no more pain and no more sorrow.

When I woke the next morning I was angry at God for my unanswered prayer. The question burned in me: *Why am I still here?*

At that moment, I received an immediate answer that

spoke to my heart, **"I love you. You are my son. I have a purpose for you and I am not finished with you yet."** It was a very powerful message to a child that was struggling with some deep abandonment and attachment issues. I was not feeling fully accepted by the world, not feeling like there was a purpose to life, or that there was a real hope for a fulfilling future. It was a dark world to live in at that young age. These divine words of comfort came as a soothing balm to a hurting soul; a message that would bear repeating at a later stage in life.

Having God state his fatherhood to me was a hard concept for me to grasp. How can I be his son? I thought Jesus was his son. I was familiar enough with the Bible to know that was true. I was adopted into the Campbell family, sharing only their last name, but knowing beyond a shadow of a doubt that I belonged to them. Yet here I was, in a moment of desperation, and I received affirmation from my heavenly Father, ensuring me of my adoption into his spiritual family, the Family of God. (John 1:12, NIV) Many years later this message would bear repeating, but under very different circumstances.

## When My World Turned Upside Down

**ON OCTOBER 11, 2001, I WAS TRAVELLING TO A MEETING IN** Listowel, Ontario. As I was about to pass a sixteen-wheeler on a dark, two-lane highway headed west, the minivan in front of me decided to do the same thing and pulled out in front of me so I had to follow him in order to pass the truck. When the van pulled in front of the truck, it did not leave enough space for my car to get in between. I was now stuck in the eastbound lane with oncoming traffic quickly approaching. I veered onto the shoulder of the road, but saw some flashing lights with which I was about to collide. Thinking it might be a horse and buggy, since this is Amish country, I swerved back onto the lane. Wanting to avoid the imminent head-on collision, I placed myself in the midst of another one with the oncoming eastbound traffic right in front of me. When I turned the wheel, the rear of my car spun out on the gravel and shot me across the eastbound lane back into the westbound lane. The trucker must have seen this transpiring and slowed down because I was now facing the truck that I had just tried to pass. With the Mack grill bearing down on me, my car continued to spin out of control and I dropped into an embankment, flipping the vehicle multiple times. The car finally landed at the bottom of the ditch, pinned against a tree.

First on the scene were an off-duty firefighter and the head nurse from the Campbell Soup factory just down the road. Although I knew I wasn't physically injured, I was still put through a battery of questions.

The nurse asked, "Sir, how do you feel?"

"Stupid," I replied. They chuckled and breathed a sigh of relief.

I was immediately deemed stable and in my right mind and was asked if I could get out of the car. I said, "Yes." But when I undid my seatbelt I hit the ceiling with a clunk. Still disoriented, I did not realize the car was upside down.

As I crawled out of the window, the kind nurse laid her jacket in the ditch and instructed me to lie still until the paramedics arrived. Still feeling like I was fully functional, I wanted to figure out how I could get to my meeting on time. This was not to be, for when paramedics arrived, they strapped me to the spinal board and hauled me out of that muddy pit; shaking their heads in amazement that I had survived the crash.

I was told I was lucky to be alive at least ten times en route to the Listowel hospital. It was also mentioned repeatedly by the nurse during the initial triage intake and the on-duty police officer who came to visit me a couple of hours later to take the accident report. The words "being lucky" played over and over like a chorus, but never really struck a chord with me. It was not until a nurse said as I was being placed in a waiting area, "Young man, you have an angel looking over you, maybe more than one. From what they tell me, you should be dead, a hundred feet from your car, but you're not and there is a reason for that . . . I don't know what it is, but there's a reason."

I was wheeled into a darkened room to wait for the doctor to assess me for spinal injury. It was very uncomfortable being strapped to the board. I was forced to stare up at the florescent lights. Every time I closed my eyes, I would see the chrome grill coming at me. I started searching my mind and thinking of what could have been. Questions plagued me. *Why was I still here? Why was I not lying a hundred feet from my car, in the ditch with a white cloth over me?* It was a sobering question and one that I wanted answered.

In that moment, I heard a still small voice say, **"I love you Thanh, you are my son and I have a purpose for you, and I am not finished with you yet."** It was like an echo from the past. I vaguely remembered hearing that before, strangely familiar, yet with a different overtone. It brought a sense of peace to me and I was able to rest there forgetting the discomfort I could not escape before.

A couple of weeks earlier, I had been wrestling with some spiritual issues and I had renewed my vows to God. Somehow this experience assured me that I was being protected and that those vows were being taken seriously.

A couple of hours later, I walked out of that hospital a different person from the one who had been wheeled in many hours earlier.

# It's A Small World

**MY FAITH STARTED TO DEEPEN IN RESPONSE TO HAVING** that particular message of belonging repeated to me. I began to understand that sharing my life story to different audiences was somehow going to be part of that ultimate purpose with which God had commissioned me. I've discovered that the desire to belong is a basic longing in everyone's heart. When people hear my story, they connect to it on various levels; some on the surface level as a good drama, but others are connected on a deeper emotional level due to some void in their own life.

I started sharing my story more frequently with groups in formal situations and upon some very impromptu requests. All of the people listening are interested and mostly all express their amazement, some are even inspired in some way to appreciate the blessings in their life. Yet most people are honest in sharing the feeling that they could never really imagine what it would be like to be me.

I have been public speaking since working at Redeemer University College in 1998. I would speak at church services and to small groups of students in their high schools promoting the university and its programs. It was preferred that I would not do a "commercial" in the service, but asked to do a bible message and then talk to people about the school after the service.

This continued into my work with Christian Reformed World Missions (CRWM), which afforded me even more opportunities to speak across the country. On my first visit to a church, I would introduce myself and share a bit about my story to provide context as to why I was involved.

In 2004, I was speaking at Second Christian Reformed Church in Sarnia, Ontario. Afterwards, I was standing by my information table talking with those who stopped to visit. Brian and Brenda Zylstra were in line that day. When they finally got their turn, they were not interested in asking about CRWM, nor the sermon I had just given. Instead, they said something that got my full attention.

"We think we know someone that was on the same plane as you when you were a baby," they said. "We work with someone and he has a very similar story to yours."

Not sure of how to respond to this, I said, "Not likely, there were a lot of kids who were taken out at that time, but I am always interested in talking to people from the same country as me." I handed them my business card to be passed on; never assuming it would ever be used. I had never met anyone else who had come over on a plane. Anyone else I met had come after the end of the war and they were part of the Boat People. It never even crossed my mind that I would be able to meet someone that flew with me in 1975, so I never tried to find them.

## The Call

**THAT FRIDAY NIGHT AT SUPPER THE PHONE RANG, WHICH** is nothing surprising with all the telemarketers around. What was unusual, however, is that I answered the call; typically we don't interrupt our dinner. After my greeting, the person on the line said: "Hi, it's Trent Kilner from Sarnia, Ontario, and I was on the same plane as you back in 1975." After hearing those words, my life would never be the same…

Trent's words rang in my ears. I was speechless. I am not sure how long the silence lasted before I replied. "How do you know?" I said, getting up from the table.

Dazed, I walked into the living room, leaving my family staring after me in bewilderment that I had even answered the phone while at the dinner table, let alone left the room.

Trent quickly responded: "Helen Allen and Victoria Leach with a team of doctors and nurses from Canada brought us out and took us to Hong Kong, to Vancouver, and then to Toronto, where we ended up at Surrey Place."

Those names, those destinations of that itinerary, were such a part of me, as much as any appendage or my dimple when I smile. I grew up knowing those names, though I had never really known the women who rescued me. The travel route was one that I had recounted so many times when sharing my story; whether it was at show-and-tell in elementary school, or more recently as a guest speaker in churches or as a keynote speaker at special events. Now, here was someone I had never met, saying he had shared the same start in Canada as I had.

I knew "they" — the other orphans — were out there somewhere, but I never imagined that I would ever have the chance to meet one. It was something I felt had made me unique in all of the circles I had ever travelled.

Trent and I decided to meet at my house and hear each other's stories. The next weekend, he was at my door with photo albums in hand. We spent the time sharing pictures and talking about what it was like growing up as Vietnamese war orphans in Canada. His parents knew Victoria and Helen very well and had stayed in touch with them over the years through the Can Adopt organization, which was why he was so well versed in our trip to Canada.

Trent's adoption experience was very positive, much like mine. The Kilners had some of their own biological children and then adopted Trent. But unlike the Campbells, Trent's parents continued adopting kids into the family after Trent came. In total, he has twelve siblings. I eventually had the chance to meet his parents and some of his siblings down in Sarnia.

As we got to know each other more we found out that we also shared some of the same ways of thinking when we first arrived as children. Trent's father, Earl, shared a funny story about Trent that showed that we were even more alike. Trent, too, was known to work out of a scarcity mentality. During his first year in Canada, his mom, Gail, would clean his room and discover caches of food — from fruit to sandwiches. It did not take long for his parents to figure out that he was hoarding food. As an experiment, Trent's father placed a full box of Ritz crackers in front of him and witnessed his young boy hastily eat the whole box in one sitting, as if fearing someone might take it away from him. Moved by this sense of panicked eating, the Kilners sat Trent down and assured their new son that now that he lived in Canada, there was plenty of food and he needn't worry about eating so much at once, or hiding food for later.

Trent and I became fast friends and considered each other the closest thing to a Vietnamese "family." It was great to have a counterpart in this world that understood a part of me that no one else ever had. Meeting Trent helped me resolve that perception of *no one would ever understand me; no one really gets me.* Proud as I was of telling the heroic tale of risk, rescue, and love that brought me to Canada, there was never a feeling of being fully understood by anyone I had ever meet before him.

chapter 6

# The Plot Thickens

**AFTER TRENT AND I MET AND HAD BEEN CORRESPONDING**
for while, with the help of his sister, Heather, we started
digging around in the National Library and Archives by
Queen's Park. We were trying to find out as much
information as possible about our arrival into Canada. We
were able to find a number of news articles that had been
written about our group and discovered there was another
flight that arrived before us, but it had flown into Montreal.

We discovered that the other flight had about the same
number of passengers, but was spearheaded by aid workers
Naomi Bronstein and Helke Ferrie. Victoria Leach and
Helen Allen had met these women during their brief stays
in Saigon earlier in 1975. What this told us was that there
were more orphans out there who started their life in
Canada the same way we did, they just landed in a different
province. Where these individuals went, we weren't sure,
but we are hoping for the chance to swap stories with
them someday.

Through the news articles we found out that this group
of orphans had met together with Naomi many years later
and maintained a connection with one other. We also
discovered a story of fifty-seven orphans who had been

blessed by an airline company in the United States that organized a trip to take the group back to Vietnam for a tour and rediscovery of their origins. We were envious to say the least, but inspired that perhaps we could do the same for our group.

We started mulling over the idea of what would it take to meet the others who were on our flight. *How could we reach such a potentially vast diaspora of immigrant children? How would they even find out we were looking for them?* After a few weeks of researching we began to realize the answer was staring us in the face. In all our searching for official government documents about our flight and adoptions, we were left holding a pile of dated newspaper clippings from all over Canada. That was when the proverbial light went on — *let's use the media!*

Our first inclination was to go to the TV stations, but we wondered: even if we did on TV, how would people get in touch with us? So we decided to build a website that had an email address that people could connect through. We didn't have a lot of contacts in the media world, but Heather knew someone who worked for Citytv.

## The Best Toonie Ever Spent

**DURING ONE OF OUR MANY TRIPS INTO TORONTO TO VISIT** the archives, we stopped into MuchMusic with the hopes that one of Heather's friends was still working there and could potentially get us on the breakfast show as a personal interest story. Unfortunately we were not able to get connected to anyone.

While we were exiting the iconic Citytv building on Queen Street, we were joking around about the people who walked into the photo booth just outside the building to either rant about some issue or share a funny story on Speaker's Corner. Speaker's Corner had been around since 1980s, and I remembered watching the show in high school. It seemed like a world away when I lived in New Brunswick and here I was standing beside it.

It was as if lightning struck the three of us at the same time and we scrambled to get a marker and some paper. Someone was gracious enough to give us a red marker and a clean piece of white paper. We quickly wrote down our website address: www.57Orphans.com. Feeling a bit awkward, Trent and I entered into the curtained box together and slipped our toonie into the machine. With the camera rolling, we started our segment, introducing ourselves, briefly sharing our story, and inviting anyone who was a part of our flight to contact us through our website. Not sure of the results it would have, we left the experience behind us and went about our quest.

57 Orphan reunion.

chapter 7
# Where Are the Others?

**TRENT'S SISTER, HEATHER, WISELY SUGGESTED WE TRY TO** track down Victoria Leach, since we knew where she had worked. We called the Ministry of Community and Family Services' office. They knew of Victoria Leach and spoke fondly her, but said that she had retired long ago, which we had assumed would be the case.

Heather was persistent. She asked if they had any way of contacting Ms. Leach and explained why we were trying to reach her. A few days later, Heather received a call from the Ministry letting us know that Victoria was overjoyed to learn that we were trying to locate her and that she had always wondered where "her children" had ended up. She explained she would love for us to come visit her at her home in Toronto's Rosedale neighbourhood and left a number at which we could reach her.

When we made the phone call to Victoria directly, she received us warmly over the phone and set a date later that month in April of 2005 when we could come and bring our families to meet her. She assured us she longed for this event and eagerly anticipated the day when she would see us with her own eyes.

Armed with this bit of news, we continued on our quest to gain media exposure. We called the *Toronto Star* and were patched through to journalist Jordan Heath Rawlings. We told him who we were and about the story that had been covered in 1975 by his newspaper and offered a good news follow-up story about the reunion. This time the media was interested.

Next we called the Canadian Broadcasting Corporation (CBC). It had covered the arrival of the Vietnamese orphans in Vancouver and our landing in Toronto. They leapt at the chance to report a good news story, assigning the story to journalist Mellissa Fung (now famous for her own harrowing tale).

When the Kilner and Campbell clans met for the first time, it was in the parking lot of the Rosedale condo where Victoria Leach lived. We knocked on her door and when it opened, we were met by camera flashes from the newspaper photographer. A small women stood silhouetted at the door with her arms extended to greet us with hugs and handshakes. Thirty years' worth of tears of joy were shed.

## Found

WE ALL HUDDLED AROUND VICTORIA AND LISTENED TO her recount the stories of flying into Vietnam during the spring of 1975, assembling the team, and the eventual last flight out. It had been the goal of the team to rescue 500 orphans, but when they got to the orphanage, the care-workers could only prove that fifty-seven of the children were "true" orphans. As she was recounting the story, the photographer was busy sorting through archival images of our arrival at Surrey Place. At one point he held up a black-and-white photo and declared, "I found you, Thanh!"

Every head in the room turned to look at the picture. "That's you!" my dad exclaimed. While the picture was being passed around, my sister said: "I remember that sweater," and stated that if my head had been turned the other way, she could have confirmed it was me because my ear is flopped over at the top.

Reluctantly, we ended our visit with Victoria Leach. We said our goodbyes and had a brief meeting in the parking lot with the media, who thanked us for sharing this opportunity with them.

Three days later, the story hit the airwaves; first with the CBC's "The National" with Peter Mansbridge. Though it was surreal to hear him speak our names on national news, this was just the beginning. The *Toronto Star's* Mellissa Fung and her team put together a heart-warming video documentary about Trent and I discovering each other and the reunion with Victoria Leach.

The next big media story came on Sunday, April 18, 2005. My sister Nancy was living in PEI at the time. Before church that morning, people were stopping by her house to show her the picture on the cover of their Sunday edition on the *Toronto Star*. They were inquiring whether she thought the picture resembled her brother from Ontario. When she looked at the image, she saw on the front page a full-page picture of a little Vietnamese boy with the number "32" pinned to his sweater. The caption read, *Where Are The Others?* She picked up the phone and called me. "Hi Thanh, its Nancy. Why are you on the cover of my morning newspaper?" We had a good laugh as I recounted the week's events.

## Here We Are

**FROM THAT POINT ON, WE WERE RECEIVING CALLS FROM** various media outlets asking for interviews and for Trent and I to come on their shows to share our story. Victoria Leach was asked to join us on "Canada AM." With so many interview requests coming at us, Trent and I had to divide the opportunities and decide if we were going to team up or go it alone.

A week after the news stories aired, we started receiving messages to our 57 Orphans website. Other orphans who had flown with us were coming out of the woodwork and we started making connections we never imagined were possible. Some of the orphans were living in the immediate region; others were in northern Ontario, out-of-province or in different countries, but they contacted us to let us know about their existence and whereabouts. Eventually, we were meeting these new friends face-to-face and building some great connections as we recounted our personal stories of adoption and integration into Canadian society, which, for the most part, were positive experiences. As our network grew, we started doing news stories of the latest reunion of orphans. It was beginning to be quite a collection of newspaper articles and TV news stories. We started meeting regularly as a group for various occasions, such as Flag Day in Toronto's Nathan Phillips Square or just for an evening on the town with new-found friends.

# The Reunion

**AS THE NUMBERS INCREASED, WE ALSO STARTED GETTING** organized for a larger reunion gala dinner. A date was set for April, 2006, and we sent out invitations to all of the orphans and their families. To our great pleasure, we received inquiries from those who were part of the now-famous flight, from the volunteers at Surrey Place to the pilots who flew the Hercules C150 out of Saigon, as well as our VIPs Victoria Leach and Helen Allen. We put together a Gala Event Committee that met regularly to plan the special event.

We decided to create special plaques that we would present to those individuals who we wanted to thank for their heroic efforts in bringing us to safety. Surrey Place Centre opened their doors for a tour and the Ontario Provincial Government opened one of its meeting rooms to host a meet-and-greet and luncheon afterwards. We felt honoured and grateful for all the support and encouragement being sent to us by Canadians who read our story in the media and those who were coming onboard to make the Gala a reality. We owe a debt of gratitude to them all including the staff at The Oakville Conference Centre in Bronte, Ontario.

On Friday, April 15, 2006, we started the event. We had a casual meet-and-greet as people came in from out of town. Throughout the evening, the orphans were introduced to each other and we had the opportunity to meet the families, friends, and extended families that had come with them. We also had the amazing opportunity to hear the personal account of the flight out of Saigon from the Air

Force Pilots, Cliff Zacharias and Bob Nicholson, who had risked their lives to rescue us. They had made a special poster and had a copy for us all that included a special article written by Cliff, a photo of the pilots in their regiment, and the log report of their flights into Saigon. After they dropped us off in Hong Kong, they said they had always wondered what the future had held for us. They were very pleased to have been invited to this special reunion.

We had the chance to hear from other special guests that night. We heard stories from the stewardess that flew on the Air Canada flight from Vancouver to Toronto and many of the volunteers at different points in our journey who had witnessed how sick we were and the miracle that we had survived.

The following day, we headed down to Surrey Place Centre in Toronto and received guided tours. We were taken to the area where we had been quarantined. Some of the orphans and parents remembered the place, but for most of us it was like seeing it for the first time, trying to imagine what it was like to be there as an infant, toddler, or even a young child.

Our parents shared heart-warming stories of the moment they met their adopted children. There was my family, the Campbells, who came on April 18 to pick me up. Trent's family, the Kilners, on the other hand, had travelled from Sarnia but were turned away, as no more children were being released until they reach a margin of health. It was not until six weeks later that Trent was allowed to go home.

The staff who had worked at Surrey Place during that time recalled what it was like taking care of the sick children. They required twenty-four-hour care and each volunteer that came in was assigned the same children to work with so that nothing that was communicable would be transferred amongst the children, nor the workers.

On Saturday night, we had a wonderful celebration with dinner and presentations to some of the significant people from this journey. Many expressions of thanks were made to our adoptive parents and caregivers. Many tears of appreciation, joy, love, and laughter were shed. It was a milestone event that those who attended will not forget.

A very precious moment was when my friend Khanh Ho and his father came to the front in full Vietnamese cultural dress. Khanh would translate his father's words. His father welcomed all of the orphans into the Canadian Vietnamese community and declared we were "orphans no more" as he welcomed us as part of their family.

The media had yet again come through for us and covered the story of the reunion. We were interviewed on "Canada AM" the next morning with Cliff Zacharias, the captain of the Hercules plane. Daily newspapers hosted photographs that captured the joy of old friends reuniting and new friends finding one another after a long separation. It was a celebration that we would long remember and cherish. The media coverage secured that it would go down as a great moment in Canadian history.

Upon reflection shortly after the event, we realized it was going to be the best story we would get to share for a long time and a way for the group to connect to their past and to their origins. A lot of questions got answered and some gaps in our stories were made clear. It was probably the closest thing we as a group would ever get to know about our heritage.

Trent Kilner

Thanh, Trent and Surrey Place Staff

Khanh Ho, my first interpreter.

**PART THREE**

# LOST AND FOUND
## Toronto to Ho Chi Minh City
## April 21, 2006 to June 2009

Journalist Thanh Truc
and Mai Lai

Tuan Lai

chapter 8
# Email Scam or What?

**AFTER THE EXCITEMENT OF THE REUNION HAD DIED DOWN,**
life went back to normal . . . for a week. On April 21, 2006,
I received this email from a journalist in Vietnam:

> Dear Mr. Thanh Campbell,
>
> I am Thanh-Truc, reporter from Tuoi tre
> (Youth) press, one of the leading newspapers in
> Vietnam with circulation of over 400,000
> copies/day. I learned your email from Dana Borcea
> (The Hamilton Spectator). I've read that you were
> the co-ordinator of the reunion of Vietnamese
> orphans in Canada after 31 years. I would like to
> contact you and the people who were there in the
> reunion for more information. I also learned that
> some of you are planning a trip back to Vietnam.
> I believe you have interesting stories to share
> with Vietnamese readers. It would be a great
> honor if your stories come out right on 30 April,
> the reunification day of Vietnam.
>
> I am writing to ask for an interview with you
> and contacts of other people that I believe you

may have (such as Tuyet Yurczyszyn , Kilner,...) . I shall send the questions to you as soon as I get your confirmation.

Many thanks and best regards

-----------------------
Thanh Truc Nguyen (Miss)
World News reporter, Tuoi tre (Youth) newspaper
Website: www.tuoitre.com.vn

I couldn't believe I was being contacted by a foreign journalist. My world all of a sudden got very small. I had always talked about the country of Vietnam as my own, and I had met people who had lived there but now lived in Canada. I had never communicated directly with someone who still lived there. I was amazed that the story caught the attention of this journalist halfway around the world!

From talking to Vietnamese people who had immigrated to Canada after the war, I was aware that people in Vietnam knew of the evacuations of the orphans. During our celebration at Flag Day in Toronto's Nathan Phillips Square, we were inundated by Viet community members wanting to talk to us and congratulating us on finding each other. Yet I didn't expect a journalist in Vietnam would eventually be writing an award-winning article to tell the nation of our happy turn of events in Canada.

Thanh Truc told me that she was drawn into the story she had found online and her heart was filled with an immense need to share it with her countrymen. She asked for permission to rewrite the story and publish it in Vietnam. She said people there had always wondered "what happened to their kids." It was heartwarming to think that we were missed by our people.

In July, Thanh Truc sent me the story she had written — but it was in Vietnamese! Since I don't read the language, I had to ask her to have it translated. I received a second, translated version and was satisfied with her understanding of and perspective on the story.

A week after the story was published in Vietnam, I received a follow-up email from Thanh Truc about the story and the great response it had received.

> Hi anh Thanh,
>
> ... After the story came out, 2 people have reached me to ask for more information. One of them is an old man, whose name is Nguyen Minh Thanh. I've just talked to him 5 minutes ago and write to you immediately.
>
> He said he had a son whose name was Nguyen Ngoc Minh Thanh, born May 1st, 1973. He had to temporarily give his son to the Go Vap orphanage because he fought for the Saigon military [South Vietnamese] at the moment. His son was taken away on babylift campaign in 1975 and he has been trying to look for him ever since. He showed me a copy of his son's birth certificate, the same one of which was tied to his son's wrist when he was taken away.
>
> He was not sure whether you are his son or not, but he believed in his intuition. I hope you still have yor personal document and birth certificate. Please check if it matches. It's almost

11 AM now in VN, which means it's 12PM in Canada so I can't call you. I'll try to reach you this evening to talk to you more.
Cheers
Thanh Truc

A few days later I received an email via the 57 Orphans website.

Dear Mr Thanh Campbell!
    My name Nguyen Ngoc Minh Thao
    My father Nguyen Minh Thanh,
    My mother Nguyen Thi Ngoc Thu
    we live in viet nam.
    My family have got a member like you
    His Name Nguyen Ngoc Minh Thanh, we couldn't contact with him since 1975, he left Viet Nam in the Babylift project when he is a child
    After 30 year, and nowadays my father always to find the information about him.
    My family and I have read the Tuoi Tre Magazine yesterday (Saturday, 15/07/206) Evrybody see you very very like my brother, Now, I can not tell with you some thing.
    My father stil keep Thanh's Birth Certificate
    And we are contacting with Miss Thanh Truc to contact with you.
    If you have some infomation like that ,please contact with us,
    My father very very happy when he read the Tuoi Tre Magazine ,

I am waiting for you.
Nguyen Ngoc Minh Thao.

Though I did not need to, I pulled out the birth certificate that had accompanied me to Canada in 1975. It was still in the same envelope with the other papers that Joan had given to me when I was thirteen. I had memorized the names on that paper, but I wanted to make sure my eyes weren't playing a trick on me. When I read the names, my mind started to spin and my heart started beating faster. How did someone I did not know have those exact names at their disposal? I was very skeptical and scared that I had left copies of this paper at a presentation and now someone was playing a cruel Internet prank on me — not funny!

## Canadian History Books

THE INTERESTING POINT ABOUT THIS STORY IS THAT Trent was in the news just as much as me. It is also not out of the realm of possibility that if Ms. Truc had not heard back from me, and gotten in touch with Trent instead, the story and photograph published in Vietnam would have been about him.

In fact, many of the media articles published locally were about the other orphans getting together. I was not able to attend all of the smaller events leading up to the reunion. The orphans' story was picked up by a journalist in Sarnia, Ontario (Trent's hometown), and subsequently published in a high school textbook and integrated into Canadian history studies.

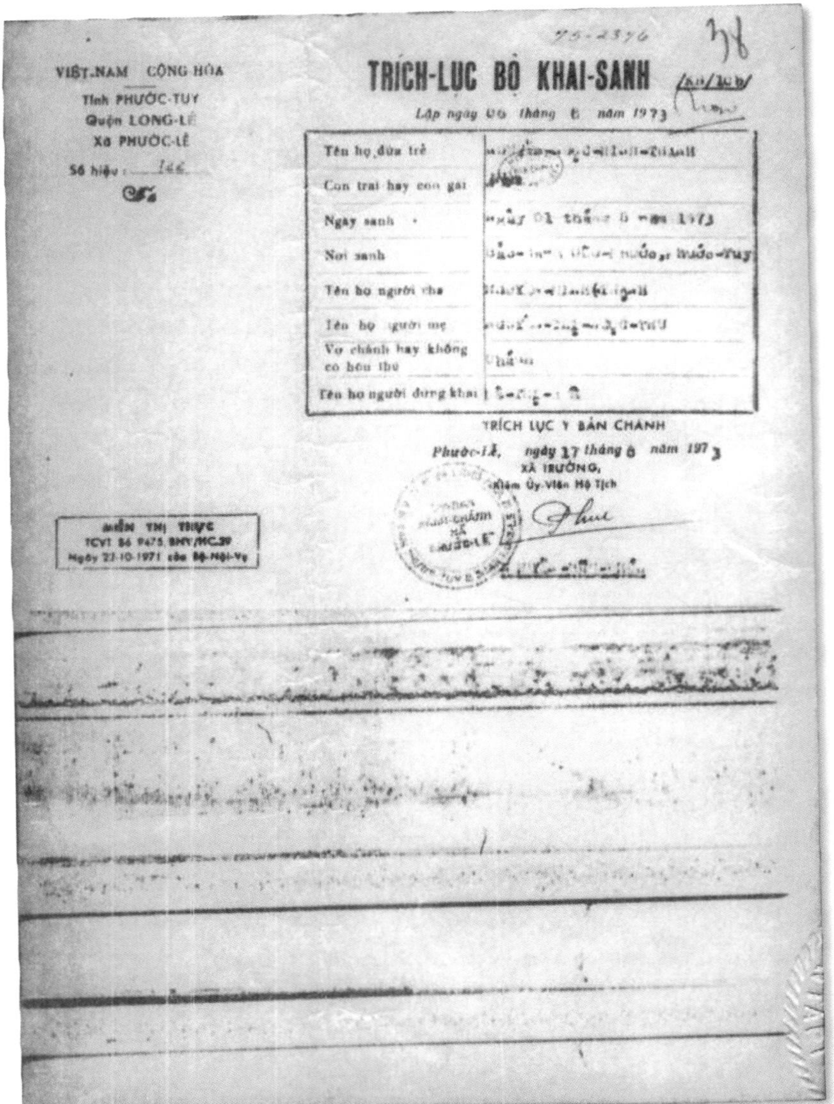

VIỆT-NAM CỘNG-HÒA
Tỉnh PHƯỚC-TUY
Quận LONG-LÊ
Xã PHƯỚC-LÊ
Số hiệu : 144

# TRÍCH-LỤC BỘ KHAI-SANH

Lập ngày 06 tháng 6 năm 1973

| | |
|---|---|
| Tên họ đứa trẻ | [illegible] |
| Con trai hay con gái | [illegible] |
| Ngày sanh | ngày 01 tháng 6 năm 1973 |
| Nơi sanh | [illegible] |
| Tên họ người cha | [illegible] |
| Tên họ người mẹ | [illegible] |
| Vợ chánh hay không có hôn thú | [illegible] |
| Tên họ người đứng khai | [illegible] |

TRÍCH LỤC Y BẢN CHÁNH
Phước-Lễ, ngày 17 tháng 6 năm 1973
XÃ TRƯỞNG,
Kiêm Ủy-Viên Hộ Tịch

MIỄN THỊ THỰC
TCVT Số 9475 BNV/HC.39
Ngày 27-10-1971 của Bộ-Nội-Vụ

Original birth certificate.

39

(Ontario logo)

Ontario

Ministry of
Culture and
Recreation

REF. NO.

**TRANSLATION**

NAME: Nguyen Ngoc Minh Thanh

The following information in respect of the above named person is recorded

in    Vietnamese    on a document    Birth Certificate

issued by

at    on

submitted to this office for translation into English: —

Date and place of birth:

Republic of Vietnam
Province  of Phuoc Tuy
District of Long Le
Village of Phuoc Le
Registration number  722

EXTRACT
from
THE REGISTER OF BIRTHS

Date of Declaration: 6/8/1973

| | | |
|---|---|---|
| Child's full name | : | Nguyen Ngoc Minh Thanh |
| Sex | : | Male |
| Date of Birth | : | 1/8/1973 |
| Place of Birth | : | HUU PHUOC Hospital, Phuoc Tuy |
| Father's full name | : | Nguyen Minh Thanh |
| Mother's full name | : | Nguyen Thi Ngoc Thu |
| Rank of wife | : | First |
| Name of declarer | : | Le Thi Hue |

EXTRACT FROM THE ORIGINAL RECORD
Phuoc Le, 17/8/1973
Chairman of the Village/
Acting Civil Status Officer

Nguyen Huu Phuc

(signature)
Manager

Translation Services
Queen's Park, Toronto.
Phone 965-2891

JUN 9 1970

Translated birth certificate.

Nguyen family estate (Jasmine producers).

## chapter 9

# Who Am I?

**I RECALLED WHAT MY MOM HAD TOLD ME YEARS AGO, THAT** the birth certificate I carried probably wasn't my own. Likely there was no personal connection between me and this family. The next logical step would be to find out as much information about this family as I could. So I wrote to Thanh Truc to find out what she knew. She replied:

> Dear anh Thanh,
>     … I can ask Mr. Nguyen Minh Thanh if Nguyen Ngoc Minh Thao is related to him. I have little information about this gentleman, just as what I told you earlier, he fought for Saigon military during the Vietnam War. He claimed that he had to give his son to the orphanage for the sake of his son. The boy was then transferred to a branch of the Go Vap orphanage in Can Giuoc province because the orphanage itself was overloaded with orphans. But in 1975, all orphans were brought back to the Go Vap orphanage for the babylift campaign. A Sister who used to work at the branch told him later that when a soldier grabbed his son, she tried to explain that he was

not orphan, but still the boy was taken away. She had to tie a copy of birth certificate on his wrist. The Father who was in charge of that babylift was Pere Peter harts-Paroise de Saint Joseph-port au prince-Haiti. Mr. Nguyen Minh Thanh has tried to contact all the sources he knows, but didn't get any further information about his son.
That's all I can tell you.
Email me if you have any questions or request.

Cheers
Thanh-Truc

I had to take matters into my own hands, so I decided to email the family directly. I received an email response very quickly.

Dear Mr Thanh Campbell
     May I affirm that I just got your name — Thanh Campbell — from the Tuoi Tre Newspaper but nothings else about you.
     May I also tell you about Mr Nguyen Ngoc Minh Thanh — after we will call Mr Thanh — who we have know before so that you can match with.
     And those information of Mr Thanh which my father has been looking for and still keeps them.
     As far as, I known from my father, not just now, my father has asked his friend to put finding notice in Newspaper in the USA for a long time due to thought that all orphans by Baby lift program would be settled in America.

In 1994, when speeding up the ODP ( Orderly Departure Program) paper work with US Government, my father has reported to the US Gov about his lost child in post war and asked for help from the US Gov (please see the attached).

The reason why Mr Thanh was sent to the Orphans Care Organization is that my father worked for the US Gov, on those last days in April 1975, and when the north troops was in power in SaiGon, and to secure the safety for children, my father took refuse and temporarily sent his child to the orphans care Organization in Ba Ria – Vung Tau, Then the charity Sisters transferred them to Can Giuoc – Long An, But last spot when the Orphans were evacuate is from Go Vap, perhaps this spot the nearest one of Tan Son Nhat Airport. Nowaday, acording to my father some of the Charity sisters are still alive and inhabit in Viet Nam.

Event Mr Nguyen Ngoc Minh Thanh and Thanh Campbell are two different persons, I find that there is a simmilarity between us- One lost a child and the orther lost a family. We think that both of us have the same suffering …

Thao Nguyen.

The email came with two attachments. When I opened the first one, there was a scanned copy of a birth certificate in English with the name of the people and the name of the hospital — Huu Phuoc Maternity Hospital, Phuoc Tuy. I opened the second attachment and there was the original Vietnamese version of the document. I pulled mine up beside the screen and it looked like someone had photocopied it — an exact match. My head started to spin and something started stirring in me. A small glimmer of hope was percolating. *Could what I was told when I was thirteen years old be wrong? Imagine if this guy in the email really was my brother.* It was inconceivable!

## Seeking Wisdom

**AROUND THAT TIME, I HAD READ IN THE BIBLE, "PLANS** fail for lack of counsel, with many advisors they will succeed" (Proverbs 15:22). These words prompted me to seek counsel about this, so I started connecting with elders from the Vietnamese Canadian community we had been introduced to during the Orphan Reunion. Two key people were the coordinators for Flag Day in Toronto, Timothy Tran and my friend Khanh Ho. I told them about the email I received from the family in Vietnam. Timothy, like most of the people I talked to, was just as surprised as me that this had happened and hopeful that it would have a happy ending.

Khanh Ho was hesitant. While he appreciated the possibilities that had arisen, he warned me to be cautious. He reminded me of the great family that raised me and the wonderful life in Canada they had provided me. He complimented me on the beautiful family I had with my wife and three boys at that time.

He warned me that I did not know these people in Vietnam, who they were, or what they wanted. Even if they were true family, what were their intentions in making contact with me? Did they think that because I lived in Canada I was rich? Did they want money from me? Was it all a trick to try to get me to support them?

I appreciated his caution, but I thought about my own sons — and our child on the way. *How would I feel if one of them suddenly went missing?* I would do anything to find out where he went. I hated the thought of ever losing one of my children and never seeing him again, knowing that if one was taken from me I was helpless to do anything to get him back. It had been a fear of mine, partly due to getting lost as a child — in malls, county fairs, and once on the Halifax harbourfront. I hated that feeling and wanted to bring closure to this family, one way or another; it would also bring resolution to my mind about the whole matter.

With this in mind, I decided I would help this family prove or disprove that they had found their missing son.

I wasn't sure of my next course of action, so I called Khanh Ho again and told him I wanted to get to the bottom of this. He stated that the only way to know for certain was to take a paternity test. I laughed and asked if he meant like the ones that are done on "The Montel Williams Show." There was no way I was getting on that show . . .

## Lab Express

**KHANH WENT TO WORK ON RESEARCHING WHO COULD DO** the test and eventually he found a lab that would help us out. It was in downtown Toronto and Allan Rottenberg, the administrator of Lab Express in Toronto, was moved by the story and was more than glad to lend his services. Most of the cases he worked on were similar to the TV shows: couples arguing over custody of a child in question. This was a much better, good-news story of which he wanted to be a part.

One Saturday in December 2006, Allan came to my home in Hamilton, Ontario, to explain the process. It would be just like what I saw on the TV show "CSI" and other dramas where they needed to take DNA samples from someone. He used a cotton swab to collect epithelial cells from inside my cheek that would be used in the test. A little swipe here and a little swipe there, and that was all he needed to do. A kit was also sent to Mr. Nguyen Minh in Vietnam.

And then we waited.

# chapter 10
# 99.999%

**ON JANUARY 7, 2007, A LETTER CAME IN THE MAIL FROM** Lab Express. I opened the envelope to find a letter and a results sheet folded together. I immediately went to the results and was bombarded with all the numbers under various headings. I knew just enough to understand that there had to be matching numbers to show a genetic match. Two columns of matching numbers ran down the middle of the paper, highlighted in a red border. At the bottom the number 99.999% jumped out at me. It was a match!

A statement at the bottom of the sheet read, "Conclusion: the alleged father, Nguyen M. Thanh, cannot be excluded as the biological father of the child, Thanh P. Campbell, because they share genetic markers. The probability of paternity is 99.999%, as compared with an untested, unrelated Asian man of the North American population." There was a mark in the box beside the words: Chain of Custody can be verified.

Soon after, I received a call from Allan Rottenberg. "Hi, Thanh," he said. "I bet you're wondering what the 99.999% means."

"I think I know," I told him. "But you'll have to explain it to me."

Allan continued, "If you could fit one hundred thousand men in one room, only one of them could have the same genetic make-up as you. So in essence, Thanh, you have found your birth father — or he has found you!"

I was stunned. *How was I supposed to process this news?* First, meeting Trent was out of this world. Then meeting the other orphans was more than I ever thought would happen in my lifetime. But this was completely different. Surprisingly, something inside me shut down, almost like I did not want this to happen. My life was fine the way it was, far from perfect, but I knew what to expect on the whole. I did not know what all this would mean. I did not know these people in Vietnam. *My family lives here, they speak my language, and they know me better than anyone else.* The more I thought about it, though, I decided that I was content that the Nguyen family would receive the answer they had been hoping for. A weight would be off their shoulders. I couldn't imagine what it had been like for them, trying to find me all this time. *To what lengths did they go to look for me? Would they think it was just a coincidence that they read the article, saw my name and then made a connection? Or did they believe in a higher purpose for the events that happen to us?*

January 4, 2006

Mr. Thanh Campbell,

**Re: Case No. LEC 0597 / 10614427**

Dear Mr. Campbell:

Enclosed you will find a copy of the laboratory report addressing the biological relationship of the parties identified within, as well as an explanation of the report.

After a home visit to you at the address above where you presented photo identification in the form of an Ontario drivers licence and your Social Insurance card, I obtained your right thumb print, took an instant photograph of you and took, from you, a set of buccal swabs.

A test kit was then sent to the alleged father, Nguyen M. Thanh, in Vietnam who's buccal swabs were obtained under the supervision of journalist, Miss Thanh Truc.  Mr. Thanh's photograph and thumb print were taken. The swabs were sent to us. The two specimens, yours and the alleged father's, were then processed.

The testing has determined that there is a 99.999% probability that you are the biological child of the alleged father, Nguyen M. Thanh. The paternity index is 100,447. That means that if Nguyen M. Thanh was one of a group of one hundred thousand men, he would be the only one in that group who would have the same DNA profile as you.

These findings would indicate, with great certainty, that Nguyen M. Thanh, may be declared your biological father.

Please feel free to call if you have any questions.

Allan Rotenberg
Lab Express Inc.

**DNA TESTING**  Paternity/Child Custody/Child Support/ Immigration/ Estate Disputes
135 Antibes Drive, Suite 104, Toronto, Ontario, Canada, M2R 2Z1
(416) **DNA-TEST** (416) **362-8378**  Fax: (416) **633-0669**

## Laboratory Report

Case Number  LEC 0597 / 0614427

| | Name | Specimen # | Race | Draw Date |
|---|---|---|---|---|
| Mother | ***** | ***** | ***** | ***** |
| Child | THANH P. CAMPBELL | 10614427-2 | | Oct. 14, 2006 |
| Alleged Father | NGUYEN M. THANH | 10614427-6 | Asian | Dec. 20, 2006 |

### STR DNA ANALYSIS

| Probe / Locus | Mother's Alleles | Child's Alleles | | Obligate Paternal Allele | Matching Allele | Alleged Father's Alleles | | Paternity Index |
|---|---|---|---|---|---|---|---|---|
| FGA | ** | | 28 | 28 | 28 | 21.2 | 28 | 31.25 |
| TPOX | ** | | 11 | 11 | 11 | 8 | 11 | 1.27 |
| D8S1179 | ** | | 13 | 13 | 13 | 13 | | 3.50 |
| vWA | ** | 17 | 15 | | 17 | 17 | 18 | 0.9804 |
| D18S51 | ** | 15 | 13 | | 13 | 13 | 14 | 1.97 |
| D21S11 | ** | 32.2 | 32 | | 32 | 29 | 32 | 5.00 |
| TH01 | ** | 9 | 7 | | 7 | 7 | 9 | 1.70 |
| D3S1358 | ** | | 17 | 17 | 17 | 16 | 17 | 1.92 |
| Penta D | ** | 11 | 9 | | 11 | 10 | 11 | 2.87 |
| CSF1PO | ** | 12 | 11 | | 11 | 10 | 11 | 0.9579 |
| D16S539 | ** | 12 | 9 | | 9 | 9 | 13 | 1.02 |
| D7S820 | ** | | 12 | 12 | 12 | 7 | 12 | 2.12 |
| D13S317 | ** | 11 | 8 | | 8 | 8 | | 2.59 |
| D5S818 | ** | 13 | 11 | | 13 | 7 | 13 | 1.49 |

```
Combined Paternity Index =   100,447
Probability of Paternity    =   99.999%
```
(prior probability = 0.5)

**Conclusion:** The alleged father, **Nguyen M. Thanh,** cannot be excluded as the biological father of
the child, **Thanh P. Campbell,** because they share genetic markers. The probability
of paternity is 99.999%, as compared with an untested, unrelated Asian man of the
North American population.

☒ **Chain of Custody can be verified.**     Date  January 4, 2007

A. Rotenberg
(per Christian B. Garson, Ph.D., P.Y.C. Laboratory Co-Director)

## chapter 11
# A Very Long Distance Call

**I CALLED KHANH AND TOLD HIM THE NEWS OF THE** results. He was very pleased for he had called the Nguyen family before we did the paternity test to ask, quite frankly, what their intentions were in making contact with me. Mr. Nguyen stated very clearly that his intentions were honest and he just wanted to know if I was his son and to know that I was happy in life.

We arranged a time to place a call to the family in Vietnam. I was excited and nervous. *How is my life going to change? What will they be like? Will the language barrier hinder our ability to express what we want to say?* I was afraid that first impressions over the phone wouldn't be the same as they would be if we met in person.

I had my friend Jason Pluim film the event, just in case we needed to use the footage later on. I invited my dad and Trent and his girlfriend Lia Pouli (the youngest of the orphans that flew with us) to be there. Khanh placed the call and we waited for them to pick up the line on the other end. It felt like an eternity, but eventually someone answered. It was an older man's voice and he was speaking Vietnamese.

Khanh explained that it was my father on the line. He shared the news about the results of the paternity test and it went silent on the end of line. Then, speaking very quickly, Mr. Nguyen spoke with Khanh, telling him how happy he was to receive this news. His son Thao had received the same news as us a couple of days earlier, but did not tell his dad of the results. He wanted to wait for us to tell him on the phone. You could hear them laughing about how hard it was for him to keep the secret waiting for our phone call. He was glad he didn't have to keep it in anymore.

Nearly speechless, I stammered my introduction and explained who the people in the room with me were. I reiterated that we had got the positive results and how pleased, yet perplexed, I was to be introducing myself for the first time over the phone. Khanh relayed the message and then entered into a lengthy conversation with my birth father.

After a while, Khanh paused their conversation and translated what my father had said: "He is very happy today to receive the news. He's very touched that he found out that you are his son, that he has been looking for the last thirty-one years . . ." — I could see Khanh struggling with his own emotions — ". . . your [birth] mom passed away, and just before she passed she told him 'whatever it takes, go find him' and he's sorry your mom is not around to see the results today."

My dad, Reverend William, spoke up then so my birth father could hear. "I am sorry my wife isn't here also . . ."

Then Mr. Nguyen shared his condolences with my dad. This was so surreal for me to hear this. Here I was sitting in my living room with my two dads talking about my two moms, consoling each other and creating a bond between them. I tried to imagine my mom sitting there beside my dad with her legs crossed at the ankles, beaming at what was taking place. I wondered what my birth mother had been like and what she would be saying now if she were there.

My father expressed how grateful he was to the Campbells for taking care of me. My dad replied that it was their pleasure and that I was a very easy child to raise.

Khanh continued to translate my father's words. "What had happened to you was out of his wish. He did not want to give you away whatsoever; he has lost his blood and he is very sorry about that."

My father's side of the story was told to us. Mr. Nguyen was a high-ranking general in the South Vietnamese army and was working with the Americans. His wife, Nguyen Ngoc Thu, was so beautiful that the American G.I.s wanted her to work directly for them on the base. The Nguyens used a local Catholic orphanage as a boarding school for their children as it had a good reputation for the quality of care and education they provided. (There is a chance the other Vietnamese military personnel were doing the same with their children and that what happened to me might have happened to other children that were evacuated. There could be other parents who have the opportunity to be reunited with their sons or daughters.)

Periodically the Nguyens went to the orphanage to visit their two boys and then returned to their post. After I was born, I stayed with my parents for a year before being placed in the orphanage with my siblings.

As the war intensified in April 1975, my parents were not able to visit as often. One day in early April, American soldiers came to take children away from the orphanage as part of the Operation Babylift evacuation. Most of the children were being sent to Saigon, with their final destination being the various countries that had responded to the pleas for help. We don't know if this was prearranged by the nuns, but they had a sense of who should go and what children needed to stay.

Just when it seemed they were done, one soldier came back and took a baby from the arms of one of the sisters. She pleaded with the soldiers not to take him and tried to explain that he was not an orphan. But the soldier either did not understand what she was saying, or he did not care. As he carried the baby boy off to the waiting military Jeep, two brothers followed, caressing his head and holding his tiny hands in theirs, trying to keep him calm. They knew something the soldier did not, that their little brother had severe breathing problems and if he got too upset by crying, he would stop breathing and pass out. The brothers were successful in keeping the child calm. A quick-thinking sister ran and got some official papers and pinned them to the child's birth bracelet. The infant was passed to another soldier waiting in the back of the Jeep. As the jeep pulled away down the road, the brothers stood there with their caregivers, bewildered at what had just happened to their baby brother. Where were those soldiers taking him? Was he going to the hospital? Would he be coming back later on? And why were the nuns so upset? They did not know that when they let go of my hands it would be the last time they saw their little brother for thirty-four years.

# A New Path

**I ENDED UP AT THE GO VAP ORPHANAGE IN SAIGON. HOW** many other institutions in which I stayed en route to Go Vap is still in question. At the Go Vap Orphanage I was baptized and given a new Catholic name, Nguyen Phaolo Thanh. I was named "Phaolo" after the apostle Paul (an evangelist commissioned with bringing the Christian faith to the Gentile nations). Yet they still left my original birth bracelet on me and kept my birth papers on file.

On April 30, 1975, when Saigon fell to the Communist Regime, the war came to an end. Having lost the war and with the American troops pulling out of the city, South Vietnamese officers quickly scrambled to reclaim their children from the orphanages and plan their own escape route. For many South Vietnamese soldiers, these plans failed. The Nguyens were no exception.

When they returned to the orphanage, my parents were met with the horrific story of their baby being taken. Minh Thanh and Ngoc Thu's hearts broke, as any parents' would. Panic-stricken over their missing baby, questions of how and why came flooding down upon them as my birth mother collapsed in grief. *Where could they have gone?* Reclaiming their other two boys, Thuan and Thien, they left as a broken family, trying to comfort each other from an irreversible pain that would linger for decades.

# The Mission

**IMMEDIATELY AFTER LEAVING THE ORPHANAGE IN BA RIA** with their family, Minh Thanh and Ngoc Thu started on their quest to find their missing son, stopping at other orphanages and hearing the same story of American soldiers coming to take children to the city. When asked where the soldiers were taking the children, the orphanages replied, "to America."

Soon after, Minh Thanh was captured by the Communists and placed in a re-education camp as a prisoner of war. His downtrodden wife was left to fend for herself and her two boys. After two years, Minh Thanh was released. The family was relocated to the border of Cambodia and Vietnam. This was a strategic move by the Communist government so that if foreign invading armies came, there was a border community that would act as a stop gap before they could infiltrate the interior.

The family was forced to survive off the land and anything they could scrounge up to make shelter and find to eat. Their son Minh Thao was born at this time, which added to the desperation of their situation. It was many years before it was safe for them to return to Saigon, which had since been renamed Ho Chi Minh City. It was named after the North Vietnamese dictator.

They settled in the city and started rebuilding their lives. They established a convenience store that served food and drinks. Their second eldest son, Thien, eventually took over the business and it continues to be run by his family today. The eldest, Thuan, went into the construction business and continues to work in this field.

The youngest son, Thao, went to school and eventually moved on to study at college and university. He held a prominent position with the city's hydro company before moving on to work for the Intel Corporation making microchips for computers.

While they were living off the land in the jungle between Vietnam and Cambodia, Mrs. Nguyen was attacked by disease stemming from the chemical residue left by Agent Orange and Napalm used during the conflict that then seeped into the local watershed. She developed pancreatic cancer and in 1987, after only a short time in the city, she died.

Mr. Nguyen remembers her last moments. His beloved wife, Ngoc Thu, looked up at him and pulled him close to deliver her final wish. "Keep looking for our baby, keep looking for our little Thanh, never give up, never give up . . ." Weeping, he held her and promised he would never quit looking for their lost son, Nguyen Ngoc Minh Thanh.

Her sons say that their mom did not die of pancreatic cancer, but of a broken heart over her lost baby boy.

Although Minh Thanh eventually remarried, he kept his promise to his first wife. One day in 2005, he caught wind of a news article about Vietnamese American adoptees that were coming back to see their homeland. They were going to be staying at hotel in Ho Chi Minh City. *This could be my chance to get more information, maybe even meet my long lost son,* he thought. But instead of the help he hoped to get, Mr. Nguyen was stonewalled and denied access to the Ameri-Asian cohort. It was almost as wrenching as the first time he lost his baby, to come so close and then be sidelined. Would he ever find his son? He believed there was a God out there that knew where his son was, but wondered if his son knew that he had a family that longed to see him. Did he know that he had had a mother who died of a broken heart and brothers who lived with the guilt of letting him go with those soldiers? It seemed a very distant possibility that they would ever find him.

# No Way Out

WHEN I WAS EMAILING WITH MY BROTHER THAO YEARS later, he sent another document along with my birth certificate. It was the Nguyen family's application to come to America in 1994. As a last-ditch effort, Minh Thanh began his application to the Humanitarian Operation (HO) program to try to get out of the country and move his family to the United States. The HO program was a refugee program set up to allow Vietnamese who had worked with the U.S. Army during the war to come to America. As part of the application Minh Thanh wrote this statement:

> I have a child named Nguyen Ngoc Minh Thanh (male, born May 01, 1973 in Phouc Tuy Province) who was brought by the American to go abroad during the days before April 20, 1975, location of departure was Can Giuoc Orphanage (Managed by Cho Quan Monastery) and the trip guidance was Pere Peter Harts — Paroisse de Saint Joseph — Port au Prince — Haiti, but up till now I have still not found him yet.

His application was denied — it was another devastating blow. *What was left to do?* There seemed to be no path left open to him. Only his prayers and faith kept the pilot light on, simmering hope that one day a wonderful reunion would take place. *Only by God's providence could this happen,* he kept assuring himself. Every year on January 2, the anniversary of his wife's death, the family would visit Ngoc Thu's resting place and he would recommit himself to her plea. He would not give up, nor would his faith let him.

# A Voice In The Night

**IT WAS MINH THANH'S FAITH THAT KEPT HIM SEARCHING.** On July 15, 2006, he came across this article in his newspaper, *Tuoi Tre*, written by journalist Thanh Truc:

### Longing for coming back to Vietnam

Thanh Campbell couldn't recall how he was brought to Canada. All he can say, from what his foster parents told him, was that he and 56 other orphans were taken to a military aircraft which left Vietnam on a chaotic day by the end of April 1975 on a "babylift" campaign. He was only 1 then.

On arriving in Canada, Thanh and the other children, from 10 days to 8 years old, were adopted by Canadian families. They had new names: Thanh Campbell, Tuyet Yurczyszyn, David Hobson, Trent Kilner... They grew up in different families, led different lives, but bore the same question: Who am I and what my life was before the aircraft took off?

Unfortunately, they had no clues for the answers, except for some orphanages that nobody knew whether still operating or not. Thanh Campbell now lives a happy life with his wife and three sons. "When I was a child, I realized my different origin and always wanted to know about my blood parents. However, my foster mother didn't hide the truth saying that they may have died in the war. All of us must be proved orphans before being taken to the aircraft." - said Thanh.

Thanh was not the only one. Most of the other children on the same flight had little or no memories about Vietnam. Thanh said in his email: "If it's possible, help me find the orphanage in Go Vap and take a photo of it for me. I'd like to give it to my friend, who was one of 57 children on the same flight with me." We know how meaningful a picture of the orphanage is to Thanh's friend.

The man Thanh mentioned is Trent Kilner, 34, a carpenter and building worker. Trent spent several years seeking information on the Internet about the 1975 flight and other children in order to find out his identity. Trent came to see Thanh 3 years ago after having heard about him from a friend. "We felt a strong tie when we first met!" – Thanh said. They are looking for an organization that helps funding for DNA test to see if they are blood brothers.

The reunion between the two men urged them to find all the people on that flight nearly 30 years ago. After their story had been published in Canada media, they found 41 out of 57, along with most of the medical staff, volunteers and pilots. And last 14 April was an unforgettable day for 33 orphan-adults when they first met after 31 years. It was destiny that had brought them on to the same flight, now it's also destiny that reunited them. Thanh said the reunion was really emotional. It felt like they were reuniting with their own relatives. Everybody couldn't restraint their tears, the happy tears of reunification.

Thanh said the reunion had strengthen the decision of some people to come back to Vietnam.

They were eager to visit the orphanages, some hoped they could find their relatives. Thanh expressed his interest when I told him about the trip back to Vietnam of the US babylift last year. "We are planning to take a trip back to Vietnam as a group, but we couldn't do it right now due to lack of funding. Everybody is longing to come back to Vietnam now!"

Khanh Ho summarized the story for us while Mr. Nguyen recounted the story of reading Ms. Truc's article.

*One day when I was reading my morning newspaper, the* Tuoi Tre, *I read about a beautiful story of two Vietnamese orphans getting together in Ontario, Canada, and then meeting the others that flew out with them along with the doctors and nurses that accompanied them. It was a beautiful story. I was so happy for them, that after so long they got to meet each other. I drank my orange juice, folded the newspaper and went about my day as usual. I went to bed that night and I woke up in the middle of the night to a voice that said, "This is your Thanh!" My mind immediately recalled the article I had read earlier in the day. One of the names of the two orphans that met was Thanh! Could it be? I could not sleep the rest of the night so I waited to call my son Thao in the morning. When he answered, I told him about the article and that we needed to find out who this Thanh Campbell is. Thao was not sure at first what to do, but then suggested they start with journalist who wrote the story.*

*We contacted the* Tuoi Tre *newspaper and got a hold of Miss Thanh Truc. She explained that she had never met Mr. Campbell, but had found him and his story on the Internet.*

*"All you have to do is put his name in Google . . . He is everywhere . . ."* So we went to the Internet and we found him. That's when I had Thao email him. We had to know if there was any connection to our little Ngoc Minh Thanh and this Thanh Campbell we read about in the newspaper.

The same morning that Mr. Nguyen called Thao to find out more about this article, he received a call from his sister who had also read the newspaper article and saw the photo that accompanied it. "Brother, who is this Thanh Campbell that I read about in our newspaper? He has our nose!" It must be a very prominent trait in our family as other people who read the article were starting to tell Thao how he looked like the guy in the picture.

## Con Thuong Ba Lam

**WHEN OUR INITIAL PHONE CONVERSATION WITH MY** father in Vietnam was coming to an end, Khanh asked if he could teach me something in Vietnamese. *"Con thuong ba lam,"* he said. I didn't know what it meant, but I repeated it. *"Con thuong ba lam."* Khanh said, "You are saying, *'I love you, Daddy.'"* Though I was nervous about my pronunciation of these very important words, Khanh prompted me to say them into the phone. *"Con thuong ba lam,"* I told my father. It went silent on the other end.

Khanh translated my father's response, "Thank you for that gift. It was a blessing. I closed my eyes and envisioned my little toddler struggling with his words, reaching out his arms for a hug and saying: *I love you, Daddy.*"

Go Vap orphanage workers prepare food for the children.

A worker prepares rice for the children at the orphanage.

Workers wash dishes at the orphanage which was also a TB hospital and an old folks home.

Lunchtime for the children of the Go Vap orphanage. 1975

Orphan 32

Babies being fed at the Caritan Nutrition Centre Saigon.

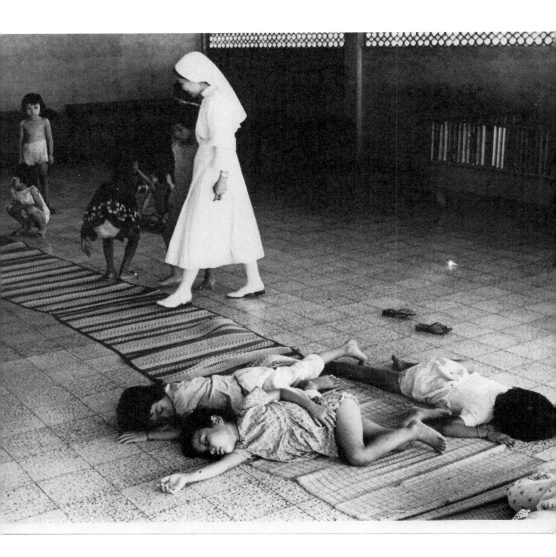

Children napping at the Go Vap orphanage.

Orphan 32

chapter 12
# The Flight of a Lifetime

**I KNEW WHAT HAD TO BE DONE NEXT. I HAD TO MEET MY** father and brothers in person. It took us almost a full two years after our phone call in January 2007 to get Vietnam-bound.

The biggest obstacle was raising the funds to get there. So, in June 2008, we held a benefit concert at the Joshua Centre in Hamilton, Ontario, hosted by Ace and Joy Clarke and their daughters, Faith and Rebekah. Friends and family came out to support the event. Artists like Faith Clarke Simms with her angelic voice and CJ Calvert, a very gifted pianist, offered their talents to help draw a bigger crowd. I had been a fan of Winona Strikwerda, Jacob Moon, and Matt DeZoete for a long time and was very pleased to hear that they were all willing to contribute their talents to the artist line-up. The cherry on the top was securing my friend Herbie Kuhn, the Voice of Toronto Raptors, as MC. We raised almost three thousand dollars that night.

We enlisted a number of travel agencies to search out the best-priced flights, knowing it would be very expensive to send me, my family, and Khanh Ho as interpreter to Vietnam.

At the last moment, Khanh could not make the trip. But he suggested a missionary couple from Chatham, Ontario, take his place.

Tuan and Mai Lai had made frequent trips to Vietnam, in part sponsored by their home church. They operated a mission that supports pastors and Christian leaders in South Vietnam. They agreed to be my interpreters.

A few months before our departure, I was visiting with my dad and telling him how preparations were going for our trip. I felt I should offer him the opportunity to come with us, one more time. The first time we talked about him going, he had felt that his health was too poor to make the trip. But this time, to my surprise, he said he had been thinking and talking about it with my sisters, and that he would like to go. It would be a great comfort to have my dad there; he had been with me since the very beginning of this journey and was the anchor to my life in Canada.

## Trip of a Lifetime

**WE WERE OFFERED SOME AMAZING PRICES BY MACTAVISH TRAVEL** in Oakville, Ontario, and in June 2009, our party of nine headed for the airport to start our trip. It seemed irrational, but right from the beginning I was afraid that one of us would get lost. After all, we were going to the foreign country in which I already had been lost as a baby! I wasn't about to repeat history with one of my own children.

We flew from Pearson International Airport in Toronto to O'Hare Airport in Chicago. Soon, we were boarding the plane for Hong Kong . . . *This was it, we were heading to the other side of the world!*

There's something about seeing the world from a different perspective. Even when there's stormy weather down below, as soon as you break through the clouds, the sun is shining. The sun never stops shining above the clouds. It is also a lesson that I have learned in my life, it is the vantage point that one is assuming at the moment that determines what he or she experiences. So much of our life is lived from one perspective, but there is always another one. If you allow yourself to consider it, the scene is a whole lot different. It requires a paradigm shift in one's thinking.

I never thought I would find myself in this situation — being on the other side of the experience of knowing there were actual blood relatives waiting to meet me.

It was a long flight to Hong Kong with not much sleep. We arrived in Hong Kong and this time had a longer layover before boarding a plane bound for Tan Son Nhat Airport, Ho Chi Minh City (Saigon). It was only a two-and-a-quarter-hour flight, which paled in comparison to our recent fifteen-hour flight. As we started our descent, a weird feeling came over me . . . *Here I am, flying into the same airport that I had left in a Hercules C130 plane in 1975 while being shot at. I have lived an amazing life in Canada, but now I am going to connect with my life in Vietnam, as brief as it was.* This was too surreal.

I had been telling my story about Tan Son Nhat Airport for so long that I had kept this place in the context of the war. I thought of the Galaxy Crash that killed 300 orphans and workers bound for the United States; and many other stories I had heard with Tan Son Nhat Airport as a central character. Upon the descent, my stomach was very tight. When we landed, I breathed a sigh of relief. As absurd as it seemed, a part of me was glad that we had landed safely without getting shot out of the sky!

# The Thirty-Year Hug

**AFTER WE LANDED AND WENT THROUGH CUSTOMS AND** immigration, we headed for the arrivals area. As the doors opened, the warm tropical air hit us like a wall. Yet it was for only a second that the humidity captured our attention. I can only describe the scene as the kind one would see at a film screening with hundreds of people behind the barriers waiting to catch a glimpse of their favourite celebrity. Even though I knew they weren't all there to greet us, it was an exhilarating feeling to have that many people clamoring to see who was coming through the doors.

As we rounded the first corner, Tuan, who was ahead of the pack, turned on his heels and asked to take my camera so he could film what was coming next. "They're here for you, Thanh," he said. In all of the commotion, I didn't quite know who he was referring to. My wife, Karina clarified, "Your family is here waiting for you, over there . . ." She pointed to a group of men along the right-hand fence. I recognized my father from Thao's pictures. He was flanked by his sons, and holding a sign that read "Thanh Campbell." I gave Tuan the camera and quickly headed over to them.

The media was there. Bright lights from cameras were flashing faster as I moved in closer. I put my hand out to shake my father's hand. I immediately recognized Thao from his pictures, standing beside my father. We shook hands and he started speaking English, introducing his family. "I am Thao. This is Mr. Nguyen Minh Thanh, your father. Mr. Thuan and Mr. Thien." I also recognized them all from the pictures, but here they were right in front of me ... what an incredible moment. I opened my arms wide and gathered them all in for a great big group hug. We stood like that for a long time, all amazed, I think, that this day had come. There is a great photo of this moment and I have titled it, "The Thirty-Year Hug."

When we were done, I looked up and there was one young lady standing behind them. Teary eyed, she approached the fence. Thao introduced her: "This is Ms. Thanh Truc, the journalist!" My face lit up and I reached out and gave her a bear hug, saying, "Thank you, thank you, for what you have done." She was a part of this family now, like a little sister we never had.

I looked behind me and my family was all watching what had just transpired. We quickly decided that keeping the fence as a barrier between us was not a good idea, so I followed the rest of the group down the remainder of the path. The cameras followed and kept rolling. As we found each other again, I saw that they were standing with more people: their families. They had all come out to the airport to meet us. Thuan's wife and two daughters; Thien's wife, daughter, and son; and Thao's new wife, Tu. My father had brought his second wife and his youngest son, Thuan.

I started introducing my family and then we looked around to see where my dad was. He was not there. He had disappeared in a sea of people. *How can you lose a six-foot-four white man in a sea of Asians?*

No one had seen where the porter had taken him. Tuan darted down the end of the hallway and found the two of them at the end of the line. The porter was dutifully waiting with my dad for a taxi, not realizing that he was part of this large commotion back toward the doors. Upon their return, something I had been waiting a long time to see finally happened: my dad and my father met. My two worlds had officially collided.

Meeting my father.

Orphan 32

Meeting my brothers.

My two dads meet.

Aaron (10 years old) in Vietnam.

Matthew (8 years old) in Vietnam.

Joshua (4 years old) at the airport.

Rachel (2 years old) at the airport.

First family photo.

Orphan 32

## chapter 13
# Vietnam 101

**WE HAILED A COUPLE OF TAXI VANS AND GAVE THEM THE** address of our hotel. It was the official Hotel of Ho Chi Minh City — where government officials and delegates stay. Our stay was compliments of the *Tuoi Tre* newspaper.

During the trip from the airport, we were all glued to the scene outside our windows: motorcycles were everywhere, vans and trucks cut us off. It did not seem like traffic died down at midnight in this city. It was a harrowing thirty-minute drive. My kids would wave to each other from one van to another and giggle when Thao and his wife, Tu, would pull up and pass us on his scooter. "Are Uncle Thao and Grandpa coming to the hotel with us?" my son Matthew asked. At first I thought he was asking about my dad who was riding in the other van, and then realized that he was referring to his new-found grandfather. He had already accepted them as part of his family. All my kids had; they were excited to have new Vietnamese uncles, aunts, cousins, and a grandpa!

It was hard grasping the fact that I was back in Vietnam, had just met my family, and didn't feel any different inside. I wasn't sure what I should be feeling, or how things would change inside, but I thought there might be something wrong with me. It seemed like it was just another day, I seemed to be taking everything in stride.

# Family of Spies?

**THE NEXT MORNING, MY FATHER WAS WAITING TO MEET US** at the breakfast buffet. My kids started looking for the usual breakfast foods. *Where were the bacon, eggs, pancakes, waffles, and cereal?* Instead they discovered soup, noodles, mixed vegetables, and fish. Eventually we were able to get some toast and jam for the kids. The rest of us were pleased to try the local fare.

Thao joined us later and we sat and enjoyed each others' company for a while. We were able to ask my father some more questions. My father wanted again to say thanks to my dad for taking care of me and bringing me up in Canada. He was proud to meet my family and his grandchildren. He sat beside me and sometimes I think he leaned in just to make sure I was close enough. He retold the story of how I was taken out of the country and the extent to which they had looked for me at the different orphanages they would come across. He couldn't believe how long it took for him to find me, and he was very grateful for Thanh Truc's article. He was disappointed that his first wife did not have a chance to see her baby again. Dad also commiserated the fact that my mom was not alive to enjoy this reunion. She would have been overjoyed to be on this trip with us.

We were sitting for quite a while and most of the patrons had come and gone. One businessman sat just behind us, spending most of the time on his phone. Before he left, he spoke to one of the waiters. The waiter then came and stood three feet from our table, never looking at us directly, but just hovering there. I thought he was just waiting for us to finish, but other servers seemed to come and go, taking our dishes away while he stood at his post.

We got up to leave and paid the bill. It wasn't until we were outside that Tuan revealed that they were listening in on our conversation and that the older gentlemen had asked the staff to take over for him when he had to go. I hope they found our conversation interesting . . . I don't think we said anything incriminating. It's weird thinking that they were spying on us just in case we came to spy on them.

## Mr. Duc's Hotel

**WE WERE SCHEDULED TO GO DOWNTOWN AND BOOK INTO** another hotel that my brother had found for the remainder of our stay. My father had to go to work and would meet us later. The rest of the family hopped into a taxi while I jumped on the back of Thao's scooter. It was a thrilling ride, zipping through traffic with a million other motorcycles and other vehicles. I think traffic lights are there just as suggestions, yet the flow of traffic keeps going and I didn't see one pedestrian get bumped.

Thao came to a three-way split in the road and two narrow roads continued between a row of buildings, some shops, some market stands, and some open air lobbies of small businesses and hotels.

We arrived at our hotel, the Xuan Mai Hotel. It would be our home for the next ten days. The owner was Mr. Duc, and he and his wife actually hailed from Texas. He had returned to Vietnam about ten years prior and opened the hotel with the intent to serve American tourists. He would be our go-to-guy for the remainder of our trip; from ordering us the right taxi service to finding us the safest restaurants at which to dine. After every breakfast he would ask my kids what they wanted for the next day's meal and his staff would shop specifically for the type of fruit or pastries they wanted.

My father came to the hotel and then Thanh Truc arrived with a cameraman. *Tuoi Tre* newspaper wanted to video an interview with my father and me for their online news site. She also came with the recent edition of the newspaper, showing us the front page that featured a picture of my father and me at the airport and an article about our arrival in Vietnam.

## Vietnam 101

**ALMOST EVERY DAY AT BREAKFAST, TUAN WOULD BRING A** local fruit or delicacy for us from the market; some of our favourite fruits today are because we got exposed to them in Vietnam. One day, he bought a cake that they eat during Tet, the New Year's celebration. We were expecting the typical Duncan Hines with an Asian twist. To our surprise it was sticky rice with a meat filling, wrapped in banana leaves. My kids were not impressed.

One morning, Tuan hired a group of rickshaw drivers to give us a tour of the city. It was amazing to see the motorcycle capital of the world from the perspective of a rickshaw rider. The city was a place of paradox: miles of brand-new, Hollywood-style hotels beside rickety old bike shops, adjacent to outdoor vegetable markets. In front of a gigantic gated mansion, a family of six huddled on a wooden deck, eating rice from an outdoor stovetop. Every street corner had dozens of people eating rice or noodles at small tables or on the ground. Some kids had smart school uniforms on, others wore rags. There were Mercedes Benz, Jaguars, and old run-down Hondas driving side by side; new taxis beside rusted-out taxis, street merchants trying to sell their wares to business people in suits drinking coffee. It was one big odd ecosystem that seemed to run without any rhyme or reason.

We were halfway through the tour when we landed at the gates of the City Palace, now called Reunification Palace, which was the head of state for Saigon. There were crowds of people coming in and out of the gates, standing and taking pictures of the massive front gates that surround the palace. Inside the gates to the right, there are a tank and fighter jet on display. It is a very significant monument for the end of the Vietnam War.

Tuan informed us that the hotel that we stayed at on our first night was equivalent to the Pentagon. It was the military headquarters for the South Vietnamese Army back in 1975. Tuan's father had worked there. It had been taken over and occupied by the Viet Cong shortly before the palace fell to the Communist Regime. I had an eerie feeling standing at the gates where the outcome of the war was decided, knowing that a couple of weeks before its demise I had left the city.

We were taking a lot of taxis and one time on a trip downtown the taxi driver got "lost" and we stopped to get directions, but he left his meter running. Keeping our tight budget in mind, we mentioned that this was not right and that he was overcharging us. A heated discussion ensued until I realized that the 6,000 Dong we were arguing about equaled about thirty cents; humbled by this we dismissed the infraction. The exchange rate is about 20,000 Dong to one U.S. dollar. Driving home that evening we saw many taxi and rickshaw drivers sleeping in their vehicles by the side of the road. It was a silent lesson on the prosperity we enjoy in the West.

We learned a lot about the culture and norms of Vietnam that I never knew being raised in a Canadian family. The elderly are highly regarded in Vietnamese culture. My dad was always served first in restaurants and we even witnessed complete strangers helping him down the hotel stairs if they saw him struggling.

(left) Clockwise from left: Thanh, Thao, Josh, Rachel, Matthew, and Aaron

(below) In the airport with my two dads.

Orphan 32

32 years of catching up.

Nguyen Thi Ngoc Thu

Nguyen Minh Thanh

## chapter 14

# Meeting My Mother

**IN 1986, AFTER MY MOM TOLD ME ABOUT MY BIRTH PAPERS,** I grew up assuming I would never find my parents. I knew they existed and something inside of me told me they were still alive, but I never considered the possibility that there would be a family looking for me.

In the movie *An American Tale*, a little mouse named Fievel comes to America from Russia and is separated from his family during a storm at sea. His sister Tanya still believes that Fievel survived and is in America with them. At one point in the movie, the two are looking up at the starry night sky from their respective places of being "lost" and singing the song "Somewhere Out There."

I was thirteen when I brought my sister and her daughter Rebecca to see that movie. I never knew at that time how profoundly that song would affect me. Even today, when I play the song, a void causes me to cry out. There is something deep-seated in me that triggers a great sadness about being separated from my family; one that I suppress and do not let surface very often. Specifically, my sadness comes from losing a mother I never got to meet. Like in the movie, I imagined her looking up at the stars at night wondering where in the world I was and praying that she would find me.

## The Picture That Took My Breath Away

**ONE NIGHT MY FATHER ARRIVED AT THE HOTEL AND HAD A** small envelope for me. I opened it and inside there were two black-and-white photos that my father had made prints of for me. One photo was of my father and another one of my mother, taken when they were both young. He was dressed sharp and I could see some similar physical traits to me.

She was breathtakingly beautiful. It looked like she could have been a Hollywood star; from the way her hair was done to the tilt of her chin. These pictures were professionally done. It was the first time I had seen an image of her, and I was moved with a sense of regret of not having had the chance to know her. Tears welling up, I wanted to tell her that I was back home and that she could rest in peace. Instead I stood there in silence and said a prayer of thanks for a mother I never knew.

The next day, my father took us out to visit my mother's gravesite. I wasn't sure what to think, feel, or expect. *This was how I would meet my mother?* It was obvious the pain of losing her was still poignant, as he feebly knelt down and spoke to her; sharing the news that their son had been found and was standing over her with his young family — their grandchildren. It was touching to see all that he was feeling. It had been a long time since she left him with this mission to find me and here I was standing beside him. It was a bittersweet end to a lifelong mission.

Afterwards, my father burned the paper money he had received from the groundskeepers upon our entrance. It is a Buddhist tradition to pay for fake money and gold leaf and to burn it on the altar of the headstone. It was termed "Hell Money" and was explained as sending currency to the underworld so that the receiver on the other side could use it to find favour. I asked if my father really believed in what he was doing, and he admitted it was just tradition, not really part of his religious belief of Catholicism.

As I stood staring at the picture of her on the tombstone, I thought of my adoptive mom. I miss my times with her, drinking tea and talking about my day. I wondered what rituals I would have had with my birth mother. *Would she like who I was as a person? Would we have the type of relationship I had had with mom?* At that moment I felt no connection, no deep sadness for losing her from my life. When I stand in front of my mom's grave in Kirkwall, Ontario, I am flooded with memories and feelings of love and being loved. I felt more sorrow for my father, who had held on to his quest to find me.

I am no expert in the afterlife, but for a moment, I envisioned my two moms meeting in heaven. Having given them both a lot to talk about, I have no doubt it would be a long conversation.

Meeting my aunt.

## Family Resemblances

AFTER WE LEFT THE CEMETERY, MY FATHER SAID HE
wanted us to visit "Sister." I assumed we were going to
meet the nun that took care of me. We drove into the
countryside and down a long dirt road. The taxi stopped at
the end of an even longer overgrown country road that was
flanked by crops on either side. In the centre stood a gated
stone house surrounded by a big stone wall. As we
approached the home, a cute old lady greeted us with a
wave. She looked at me and pointed at her nose, then
chuckled. She pointed to my nose and then again back to
her nose. *Interesting custom*, I thought. Tuan explained that
this was my aunt who had called my father about the

picture in the newspaper. She was excited to see me and the "family nose" in person.

During our visit, we found out that this had been my grandparents' estate. Even by Western standards, the house was bigger than average. My ancestors had been wealthy jasmine tea barons who owned many acres of land around the house. My aunt had inherited the property since my Father chose to live in the city after they had been exiled. She had been married and lost her husband a few years earlier. Her children now live in the United States and they come home sporadically and stay in the quarters on the other side of the cement courtyard. I was excited to know I had family living in America, and yet saddened that I never knew it all this time.

## Time Stands Still

**THE NEXT STOP WE MADE WAS TO THE GO VAP ORPHANAGE.** It took us a while to find the right location as Go Vap is also the name of the village, so it is attached to a lot of institutions. When I got out of the van, I saw some boys in the distance crowded around the door, and it looked a lot like a picture that Victoria Leach had taken back in 1975. It was the first thing that felt familiar the whole trip; I felt an attachment to those boys with their piercing yet empty eyes. We had to leave, but it felt like we should have stayed longer and tried to talk to them.

The administration staff greeted us and gave us a tour of the place. It had multiple rooms and different wards depending on the care required. We went to the nursery first and when we walked in it felt like stepping back in time, seeing all of the cribs with babies row on row. Some were napping, others started stirring as we walked around. We got to hold and play with some of them. I looked at the names of each of them and their ages. Some had no name listed and an approximate age. Most were the same age I was when I was placed there just before the evacuation. Even though it had been thirty-four years, I felt these were the kids that I had left behind. As we heard some of the stories of how the children came to be at the orphanage, a sense of guilt came over me. I wondered why I got to be the lucky one to escape.

There was one little girl to whom my family got attached. My wife Karina carried her around for awhile and asked if we could help pay for the surgery to fix her cleft palate. It would have cost $250, but the nurses said that she was too sick to have the surgery. We were then taken to a ward with terminally ill infants and toddlers. It was very sad to see these children in their beds, not able to get up and play; too weak to even sit up. It was also difficult not speaking their language to communicate with them. But even if we could, I don't know the words that would befit the sentiment in us.

The last ward we visited held the older children who were more able-bodied and taking some kind of class. My kids took turns handing out candy. We visited with two classes and then had to leave. A sense of duty was planted in me; somehow this place and its oppressive poverty and communist government needed our help. There must be some way we could help the forgotten children of Vietnam. I found out that Tuan and Mai Lai's mission, Loads of Love, was doing just that; not only in the cities, but in hard-to-reach villages across the South.

Boys polio ward, Go Vap Hospital, 1975

# Last Words

**I SPENT A FEW MORE DAYS GETTING TO KNOW MY FAMILY** before it was time to leave. I was able to alleviate the guilt my brothers had carried with them all these years about letting me go.

When it was time to go, it felt just as surreal as when we left. I couldn't believe the trip was over. *Did my two worlds really collide like this? Did all of this really happen?* So many questions plagued my mind. If these individuals were my true family and here I was leaving them again; how did they feel about that? We had to return to our lives in Canada, yet now I had opened myself to a world to which I truly belonged. I still felt like an alien in the land.

More questions came. *Was I betraying my new family by returning to my old life? Did they think I would just forget them? How do I maintain a relationship with such a huge language and cultural barrier from afar?* It was too much for my brain to take at the time, so I would just file the questions away; some would call it burying them. I knew I would have to deal with them some time and I am slowly working through the answers as I write this manuscript.

Mustering up the courage to say goodbye to my father felt like a plane circling to land in the fog, searching for some sight lines to feel safe to approach. I knew I would either fall apart in a heap of emotions or I would be able to get through it as I did when we first met. I got through it. With a final hug that I knew was very difficult for him to end, we released our embrace. We gathered up our luggage and headed for the doors.

I was leaving Vietnam for a second time. This time it was not as an orphan with a plane load of lost children. I wasn't fleeing under duress of a military coup. I wasn't being rescued to save my life from impending doom. Yet when I turned and walked away, a new battle raged inside of me; a war cry went up. *What can I do as one person to help my family and their families, and my country? I can't do everything.* Then I remembered my purpose — I can share my story.

As I entered the doorway, I turned around, looked at my father and said, *"Con thuong ba lam."* I love you, Daddy.

# Epilogue

**SHORTLY AFTER OUR TRIP TO VIETNAM, MY FRIEND AND** interpreter Tuan Lai passed away of cancer. Mai has moved in with her daughter to help out with her grandchildren. We felt this loss deeply as this trip would have been very different without his servant heart and leadership.

The following year, in 2011, my brother Thien passed away of liver cancer; leaving behind his wife and two children. She keeps the business going with her daughter Thanh and son Thang. They are both attending school and will be graduating soon.

In 2012 my brother Thao and his wife Tu, had their first child, Hinh Alvin. Tu had the baby twelve hours before Thao had to leave for a trip to Pennsylvania for training. He is a proud daddy and wants to bring his family to live in Canada.

My nieces and nephew are continuing their college education while working to help their parents survive. I would like to see them eventually come and study in here in America.

My father has retired from working for his wife in the market and spends time with his grandchildren.

My dad still continues to marvel at the trip he was able to complete. His current health condition would not allow him to do another trip like this. It was certainly a milestone event for him.

My kids remember the trip; even Rachel who was only two at the time. Aaron and Matthew have both expressed interest in returning to Vietnam someday. Josh is undecided.

I am not sure of when I will return to Vietnam, but when I do, it will be like going home again.

## Your Turn
To share your story or to leave comments please visit:
**www.orphan32.com**

# Living an Exceptional Life

CJ Calvert is a motivational speaker and author who speaks on a regular basis to world-class organizations across Canada. He is the Founder and President of CalvertTraining, the motivational arm of Shepell-FGI, Canada's largest Employee Assistance Program. Because of his expertise, CJ has been a featured guest on Breakfast Television.

In Living an Exceptional Life, CJ Calvert will reveal the key strategies that he has developed and shared with tens of thousands of people to help them create lasting, positive change in their lives. He will teach you how to:

- Have a positive attitude
- Reduce stress in your life
- Manage your time
- Set and achieve goals
- Overcome obstacles
- Transform your body

**Living an Exceptional Life is available for purchase through www.cjcalvert.com or www.chapters.ca**

World Vision
For Children. For Change. For Life.

Give
a child
chance

Sponsor a child today.
www.worldvision.ca
1-866-595-5550

# About the Author

**THANH CAMPBELL WAS BORN IN VIETNAM AND CAME TO** canada as part of the last flight out of Saigon in 1975 with 56 other Vietnamese War orphan children. Thanh was adopted into the family of Rev. William and Maureen Campbell and became the youngest of the six Campbell children.

Thanh is a graduate of Redeemer University College. He has worked for many years in the non-profit sector. Thanh owns multiple businesses including a fundraising consulting firm. As a professional speaker he tours to speak at Fortune 500 companies and various charitable organizations. He is an avid philanthropist and serves on several committees that are focused on building stronger communities.

Thanh's story has been captured numerous times in the media. Invited to be a guest on such programs as "CBC News", "TVO", "Canada AM", "100 Huntley Street", he has had the chance to share his life story with the Nation. The 57 Orphans' story has been covered by many newspapers including the *Toronto Star*, *Hamilton Spectator*, *Ottawa Citizen*, *Vancouver Sun*, *Saigon Newspaper*, and included in the French Consulate Newsletter.

Thanh has been invited to speak at numerous groups, churches, and schools across Canada as a keynote speaker sharing his story of coming to Canada.

As the next chapter of Thanh's life is unfolding, you're invited to hear this amazing story of the value of family, life, and the power of love.

**Book Thanh now as a speaker for your next event!**

**www.orphan32.com**